Take Back *Your* POWER!

Boldly Reclaim the Best Parts of Who You Are

M. STANLEY BUTLER

Take Back Your POWER! Boldly Reclaim the Best Parts of Who You Are
Copyright © 2018 by M. Stanley Butler
This title is also available as a Missive Publishing Company, LLC product.

Visit www.missivepublishing.com or www.mstanleybutler.com for more information.

No part of this publication may be reproduced, stored in a retrieval system or transmitted in any way by any means, electronic, mechanical, photocopy, recording or otherwise without prior permission of the author except as provided by USA copyright law.

Scripture quotations marked "KJV" are taken from the Holy Bible, King James Version, Cambridge, 1769. Used by permission. All rights reserved.

Scripture quotations marked "NIV" are taken from the Holy Bible, New International Version. Copyright © 1973, 1978, 1984, International Bible Society. Used by permission.

The opinions expressed by the author are not necessarily those of Missive Publishing Company, LLC.

Published by The Missive Publishing Company, LLC
100 Centennial Place #73, La Plata, Maryland 20646 USA
1.877.447.0900 – www.missivepublishing.com

The Missive Publishing Company is committed to publishing books with a message. The company's mission reflects the philosophy of its founders, based upon Mark 13:10, *"And the Gospel must first be published among all nations."*

Published in the United States of America
ISBN-10: 1732225214
ISBN-13: 978-1732225213
1. Christian: Living: Spiritual Growth
2. Religion: Christianity: General

CONTENTS

Acknowledgement 5
Foreword 7
Introduction 9
    Purpose | Own the Baggage You Were Born With 11
    Outlook | Your Birds-Eye View of the World 22
    Wonder | You Are Fearfully and Wonderfully Made 33
    Energy | When Life Becomes Little More Than a Time Suck ... 45
    Resources | This Thing Really Is a Give and Take 56
POWER Up! 66
emPOWERed 90
Conclusion 109
Scripture References 113
Get to Know M. Stanley Butler 115
Don't Miss These Titles
    by M. Stanley Butler 117

ACKNOWLEDGEMENT

To my teachers, mentors, and leaders who
led by example in a way that
I could emulate.

~Thank you!

FOREWORD

We live in a strange time. But, if you're like me, you're probably really determined that it's going to be a *good* time for me and mine. The question that always comes across my mind is, "How many people am I willing to claim as mine?" and "What can I do to do more?"

I know the second question almost doesn't make sense at all, but that exact question has been a driver of my success for nearly twenty years. So, I read a lot of books, listened to a lot of presentations, followed the life events of respected business people and leaders, and worked for men and women who didn't know more than I did, but seemed to have something that I didn't have. What I thought I knew at the time was that in order to have success, I had to model someone else's work, philosophy, career path, etc. A little of this and a little of that can become a total mess but, somehow, I managed to pull enough of it together and, as Dr. Butler describes, take one step, then two.

I was fortunate that I took enough of those steps and that my feet were pointed in the right direction. Along the way, mistakes were made, but I came to know myself better through each stumble. It was only after I realized my value, as well as the value of what I bring to other people and companies, that I was able to have a vision of what I could personally bring to other communities.

I now claim nearly 20,000 people as mine, through my business network and community outreach. I know of the importance of reclaiming the best parts of who you are, to have an optimal impact on the greatest of people—your people. It took nearly 20 years for me to learn it, but I came to know that I too could be a respected businessman and a leader worth following, when I am true to who I am and honor the work that God has chosen me to complete.

So, I write this foreword for a compelling book, tool, and companion for so many who are like me and inwardly ask, "How many people am I willing to claim as mine?" but have no idea how to take that first, uncertain step. Dr. Butler has penned something great and let us all know that the real first step is reclaiming the best parts of who we are before we embark on lofty works of changing our world or conquering any industries. After all, we can't help anyone, until we are first partakers of the very things that we intend to share.

~ Richard Creighton, MA

INTRODUCTION

I need you to take in this statement. "You are powerful!" Take all the time you need.

It is important to know that, in this instance, your power isn't rooted in or reliant upon how much money or influence you have. Your power lies in your ability to live an authentic life that establishes legacy, positively impacts the lives of others, and gives birth to ideas and visions that replicate and expand upon your works.

I wish that I would write a book that is meant for and appreciated by everyone. However, I'm going to miss that mark with this one. This book isn't meant for everyone. In fact, it's meant for a specific person; perhaps you. Do you have a dream of being more than who and what you are? Do you have a vision of building something bigger than who you are, but your life and time are absorbed by your efforts to establish someone else's legacy? Are you afraid to step out on your own? If your answer is yes to any of these questions, congratulations, I wrote this book for you!

So, it bears repeating that you are POWERful.

Unfortunately, you have neither power nor authority over time. Every unproductive, indecisive, and wasted moment lived has a cost that you are unable to pay. The psalmist wrote, **"Your eyes saw my unformed body; all the days ordained for me were written in your book before one of them came to be"** (Psalm 139:16 NIV).

What that tells us is that life's events don't occur by happenstance. There's a plan that is in operation and each of us plays a role in its success—every moment being recorded even before they are lived. While we may not know all that is written, life, circumstance, and spiritual guidance work together to enlighten us and set us on a path that was planned before the creation of the worlds.

In a world that is constantly in a state of flux, it is up to you to create your own brand of consistency and carve out meaning within it all. Once you become aware of a personal purpose and destiny, the world becomes much more three dimensional and the possibility of fullness becomes all too evident. Suddenly, you realize that you are a leader, trailblazer, originator, and change agent. Whether you choose to accomplish your work through business, ministry, public service, or family, you will need the entirety of who you are and what you possess to achieve success. You will need to reclaim the very things that others rely upon, call upon, and associate solely with you and your name.

Money and influence are only byproducts of what empowers you. Those things that set you apart from all others, increases the value of people and organizations with which you're associated, and establishes you as difficult-to-replace are largely the very aspects of who you are that you sell to some, give away to others, and take for granted more than you realize—the best parts of who you are.

Reclaiming the best parts of who you are requires that you take back your purpose, outlook, wonder, energy, and resources. Indeed, these are aspects of who you are that make you POWERful. Striking out on your own without the whole of who you are, even with the greatest effort, will likely end in disappointment, fatigue, and frustration. If you want to know true freedom and realize the fullness of victoriously successful living and operations, be prepared to make radical inward and outward changes. You will need to boldly reclaim the best parts of who you are. It is time to take back your POWER!

CHAPTER ONE

Own the Baggage You Were Born With

"I'm traveling a road called Destiny, in a vehicle named Purpose!" -M. Stanley Butler

One of your essential attributes that gives you value is your purpose. Make no mistake, even while you were wandering through your personal wilderness, engaging in self-discovery, and wrestling with coming to an understanding of who you really are and "what is the meaning of it all", others were able to see your potential and envisioned a means of not only harnessing your gifts, talents, and skill set to advance their mission, vision, or agenda; they were able to see that *thing*—your purpose—that sets you apart from anyone else. So, that's a good place to start when reclaiming your power. Reclaim your purpose!

Don't get me wrong; no one can actually steal your purpose. However, your passion can be redirected in such a way that you lose sight of that purpose and, unfortunately, lose time—time you may never regain or recover.

Purpose is a word that is oftentimes tossed around recklessly and without regard for its big-picture application within our lives. I am a man of faith, and I serve a God of purpose. While you and I may not always know what He's doing and why He's doing it, we may rest assured that whatever He does, big or small, it fits within His purpose and plan.

Let's consider this…

Romans 8:28 reads, **"And we know that all things work together for good to them that love God, to them who are the called according to *his* purpose."** This is a popular scripture, because it's oftentimes used to encourage the hearer to press through circumstances. However, at its central point, it's not about us. It's really about God and His purpose. Once you've wrapped your arms around that reality, then you can begin the process of tapping into that purpose by exercising obedient love. After all, it's really God that's doing the work. He's just inviting us to participate in what was put into action long before we were realized.

When we consider that God's plan transcends time, past, present, and future become irrelevant and merely conceptual. He is the Master Architect of the plan of redemption and He has already known every one of us, before the worlds were created. Every man, woman, boy, and girl birthed into this world has a seed of purpose within them; God's purpose—that *thing* that we are specifically and individually designed to do to advance God's plan one step further through time.

As we travel through life, we discover what it is that we excel at naturally; the aspects of who we are that has the power to free us in the moment. This shouldn't be confused with a talent. In my opinion, God gives us talents to help make life a little bit easier. If one is fortunate enough to align their talent with their profession, then there's the greater possibility of extracting joy from the work that's done. After all, it's more than just a paycheck. It becomes an exercise and reflection of who you are. Purpose, on the other hand, might cause you to become shackled in one respect or other, but experience freedoms that are unexplainable and oftentimes misunderstood by others.

In my career, I have taken on numerous support and leadership roles within the public, private, and nonprofit sectors. I've been fortunate and have been able to glean from each of these opportunities, grow my skill set, and gain clarity regarding who I am and where I belong. My talents don't cause me to take root in any particular work, location, relationship, or affiliation. However, my purpose does.

Dr. Martin Luther King, Jr., when speaking of his purpose, stated, *"I'm just trying to do a job, and I think it's a job that has to be done. I'm not trying to do it merely for myself, or merely for my children, or merely for the negro, but for America."* What was consistent within the life and work of Dr. King was a steadfast commitment to a purpose that superseded all else and served as a driver for his work. It defined him and anchored his legacy. His life exemplified obligated action rather than an exercised choice, and it pleased him that this was so. His work was his purpose.

Baggage Claim

It was during one of my trips to Atlanta that I noticed something that changed my thinking. I, like hundreds of others, converged upon the Hartsfield-Jackson Atlanta International Airport baggage claim. As the luggage began to descend and rotate around the belts, onlookers watched intently for their bags. However, in the midst of all of the hustle and bustle of travelers entering the area, exiting the area, making phone calls and general eagerness to get on their way, the luggage became the focal point of all that was happening. Every now and then, a unique piece of luggage would present itself and catch the eyes of onlookers. Some would comment on how nice it was and others commented about the assumed cost. For me, whether the luggage drew the envy or provoked the ire of onlookers became irrelevant. What I noted is that people notice and place value upon items that they recognize as beyond their means at any point in time. How does this relate to others and how they set out to lay claim to your purpose? Let's take a closer look.

It takes time and experience to hone a craft, perfect a skill, and perform competently within a field of work. Thank God for mentors who are willing to invest time and energy to develop us from who and where we are to whom and where we could and/or should be. However, even the best of mentors cannot show you how to circumvent life's events and experiences that are designed to shape your thinking, impact your heart and attitude, direct your decisions, and add required content to your life's story.

If you've shed tears, it is your responsibility to ensure that not a single one has fallen in vain. Draw from each and every experience, disappointment, victory and loss. Recognize those things that hold the potential to break you down mentally or emotionally, crush your spirit, discourage your progress, and cause you to second-guess yourself. Also, know that even these things don't have the power to embitter or enslave you. Only you have the power to allow such an impact upon your life. It is up to you to repurpose every experience so that they become a valued piece that further equips you for your work. They are parts of your repertoire—your luggage—that you may draw from as you begin to step out into your own purpose and advance toward your destiny. Yes, the cost for these pieces is high, and that's the reason why others look on with envy and ire—because the cost is beyond their means or their willingness to pay to know what you know and do what you're capable of doing. Its value— your value—is seen by others and they'll gladly borrow, pilfer from, or take possession of your purpose if you allow them to do so.

When you consider that your purpose is greater than you are and even precedes your birth, it becomes apparent that you were born with a certain amount of *baggage*. It doesn't matter how small or innocent you were when you were born, you came into this world with all of the potential needed to fulfill your individual purpose; much as an acorn contains all of the potential of the greatest of oak trees. As you live and grow, the baggage seems to become weightier; and you become increasingly more aware of that which you carry and its greater potential.

Your baggage is specifically designed for your life's travels. One may be equipped with a duffel bag, as their purpose is found within light transitions from one location to another. Yet another may travel with more durable luggage that is designed for rougher terrains and longer excursions. Still another may find that their baggage has many smaller components and accessories for specialized articles. Whatever your baggage may be, it is for your benefit as you travel your specific road, driven by your purpose. You can't afford to not lay claim to a single piece. Every experience, setback, private victory, and lesson learned adds value as it is uniquely yours and is designed to aid in completing your specific work.

If you want to watch the withering of a man's life, cut him off from his purpose. Many marriages have failed, businesses folded, men and women left with a seemingly-unfillable emptiness—not because another person fell short, but because true purpose was set aside or never fully recognized. No amount of money or provision is an adequate price to sell that *thing* that is uniquely you and yours. It is indeed your internal jewel and it gives you worth. Lose sight of this reality, and you will be susceptible to flowery words of pimps, preachers, and corporate profit mongers. These men and women have mastered the art of influencing individuals, groups and populations of people, much like yourself, into believing that it is the destiny of others to contribute to, grow, work for, and finance a *machine* that ties them down, monopolizes their time, and generally offers little tangible return for such a great investment. Resentment is inevitable and likely to be bestowed upon someone other than the man or woman who is truly responsible—*you*.

Life is a journey. No matter how great you envision your destination to be, if you fail to observe the sites along the way, you're missing out on the fullness of what your life can be. Remember, you're traveling with luggage that is specifically designed for your travels—your purpose. So, when you're so enthralled by someone else's vision that you set aside or totally forget your own or you trade in individuality for the hope of becoming a clone of someone else's perceived greatness, you will likely overlook the exit ramps offering opportunity to step into your personal destiny. Those opportunities are only accessible by placing action behind an internal knowing that pushes you into a vein of thought and works that are divinely inspired—your purpose.

So, your resolve today should be that you will not wither and die on someone else's vine. Indeed, you are specially-designed for a purpose that is all your own. It doesn't matter how well anyone else may cook, speak, sing, counsel, draw, etc., they can't do it in the manner that you would if you've been purposed to do that thing.

Walking in power necessitates knowing and acting upon your purpose. When you fail to do so, you are relegating yourself to dragging around burdensome baggage and going through motions that will likely leave you frustrated, unfulfilled, drained, and looking outside of yourself for a means of filling a great void.

What is your "job that has to be done?" The decision to take back your POWER requires that you be free to move with boldness, intention, and divine direction. This is my challenge to you; reclaim your purpose and experience the breaking of chains that have tethered you to people, employers, religious teachings, and fears. You don't have a moment to lose, so do it today!

Reflections and Next Steps

(Keep it honest and personal)

What's your decision concerning your purpose? Are you able to identify anyone or anything that is as important as your purpose? Describe your resolve to reclaim your purpose.

_____

_____

_____

_____

_____

_____

_____

_____

_____

_____

_____

_____

Reflections and Next Steps

(Keep it honest and personal)

Who do you believe God says you are? What do you believe He thinks concerning you?

_____

_____

_____

_____

_____

_____

_____

_____

_____

_____

_____

_____

_____

_____

Reflections and Next Steps

(Keep it honest and personal)

What are your talents, gifts, skill set, and resources? Are you prepared to take ownership of each of these? Who or what causes you to place more importance on one rather than another?

_____

_____

_____

_____

_____

_____

_____

_____

_____

_____

_____

_____

Reflections and Next Steps

(Keep it honest and personal)

Are you grateful for what you've been given to complete your work? How do you feel about those experiences that have contributed to who you are today?

_____

_____

_____

_____

_____

_____

_____

_____

_____

_____

_____

_____

_____

Quote in Context~

> *"I'm traveling a road called Destiny, in a vehicle named Purpose!"* -M. Stanley Butler

This quote means a lot to me, because it speaks a truth that has been applied to several areas of my life. I look at life being a journey of sorts. For many, it's not about the destination but the journey, and that's largely true for me as well. However, my belief system promises a reward for the things that I do. In this context, I'm not trying to tell anyone to take on my belief system. I cleave to what I believe, because it has proven itself within my life. I challenge my readers to believe in *something*, and further prove that it works. My belief system provides a knowing that there is a plan in the mind of God specific to me and my life—a predetermined end. My purpose enables me to live a life that pleases God and progresses me to that predetermined end.

On my journey, I've learned lessons that have shaped my thinking, way of conducting myself, and my message. I press teachings and conversations about purpose, because it is an overarching part of each of our lives. From the context of reclaiming one's POWER, one must first reclaim their purpose—not timidly or even half-heartedly, but with boldness! The God that I serve has plans for me, and He knows those plans well. They are plans that prosper and advance me toward an expected end. This leaves me in a place of knowing and owing. Because I know that my faith and confidence are well placed, I am liberated to dream; and because I know that such a liberty was purchased, I owe God my best—my solid commitment to embody all that I was created to be and do.

CHAPTER TWO

"Misfortune is a stepping stone for genius, the baptismal font of Christians, treasure for the skillful man, an abyss for the feeble." -Honore de Balzac

So, you have a vision or a dream of a business or an organization. Perhaps, at this point, it is only a concept—makes no difference. The old maxim "plan a work and work a plan" is appropriate. For many, that simple statement is easier said than done. It's a truth that there's enough bad news and discouragement in the world to occupy your thoughts and fears 24 hours each day, if you allow it to make your mind its residence. How you respond to adversity, disappointment, and even failure will impact your effectiveness and likelihood of success. In hopeless situations, someone must declare hope.

When the dream, the vision, or the work seems impossible, someone must proclaim, and even reveal, the possibility. As you make deliberate actions to reclaim the best parts of who you are, you will need to repossess your unique ability to believe that storms are temporary, setbacks are setups for something greater, and absent the faith or confidence of anyone else, you see the finished product and end result; your special way of looking at the world—your outlook.

Am I talking about being a visionary? Well, to some degree yes, but more than that. A vision is only as clear and bright as the eyes that view it. I've known "visionaries" who fall short of being effective, because their vision isn't coupled with any type of hope. They relish in negativity, anticipate failure, and position themselves to consistently proclaim that they "knew that would be the next big ___" after someone else has put the necessary work into creating something new or different. Vision is largely based upon knowledge, research, and a consistent commitment to a specific industry, idea, philosophy, etc. Those who commit to and invest in *knowing* gain the ability to see deeper and wider within their area of interest.

Your outlook works in partnership with vision. Your outlook is your visual default—your ability to assess situations, review information, parse through data and, absent enough of any of the above to draw a conclusion, choose to believe in the most prudently hopeful outcome. You were wired that way, and your outlook on the world around you serves those who come into your presence and proximity. Employers look for visionaries, but people who are capable of instilling hope in those who interact with them bring an added value to a position, a role, and an organization that is difficult to replicate or replace. It is a unique attribute that you most certainly must reclaim before striking out on your own. So, how do you do that?

Life is a learning experience. For me, self-discovery took time, trial and error, and words of advice and guidance from those who genuinely cared for me. Nearly 30 years ago, my supervisor paid me, what I considered, a great compliment. After discussing a process, she simply stated, "You don't think like a clerk." The reality is that a clerk is exactly what I was at that point in my life—at least that's what I was being paid to be. My compensation was attached to a job classification, but it did not define who I was, and it did not pigeonhole me into any particular way of thinking or impact the way that I evaluated circumstances, events, and people. That belongs to me.

A few years later, I was visiting a new friend of mine who is an entertainer. One of her bookings overlapped with my visit, so I remained at her apartment while she sang at an area church. As the hours passed, I became hungry and decided to survey the contents of her refrigerator for something to eat. While there wasn't much food in there, what I did find was about a dozen syringes. I found this curious and not long after she returned home, I asked her, "Are you diabetic?" She responded no and asked me why I asked. I shared that I saw the syringes in her refrigerator. She then explained that the syringes were vitamin B12 shots. From time to time she would become tired as she traveled; the shots were for energy. She then said, "Thank you for not assuming that I'm a drug addict, because most people would have made that assumption." In hindsight, I realized that I never assumed the negative about what I found—not for a moment. My inquiry into the syringes came from a genuine concern for the health of a friend. What I came to discover about myself, in the following years, is that I have a unique way of looking at people and situations.

As I reminisce on the words of those who have impacted my life, I recall having a discussion with my father. It was one of those discussions wherein he was sharing his thoughts of me, as much as he was providing guidance. I'm certain that he was doubtful that I heard the many things that he said, but I did. At some point during our talk, he stated, "I don't understand the way that you do things, but they always seem to work out for you." In truth, I didn't fully understand what he was saying at the time. Now, I understand.

I look at things a bit differently than many (perhaps most) do, and because of the way that I see things—my outlook—I respond differently, plan my courses of action differently, and stay within a lane that is all my own. See, my supervisor didn't realize that my title had nothing to do with the way that I took in the world and or the response that I returned. My friend underestimated people in general (and me specifically) that negativity would overshadow the truth. And my father couldn't put his finger on what was that *thing* that enabled me to walk and function outside of the norm— my outlook.

I want to challenge you to consider your specific and unique way of looking at the world and its opportunities. I've yet to meet a successful man or woman who possesses a negative outlook. Those who continually allow their conversation, thought process, and expectation to flow from a place of disappointment, regret, and distrust poison their environment, both personally and professionally. In a darkened world, there is a need for people—perhaps you— to provide a natural light and lead with communicated vision.

Surveying the Landscape

The launch and maintenance of a sustainable business, organization, ministry or even a movement will require that you emerge as a leader with something different to offer the world than what's already available. It's a truth, we live in an age where there are economic, political, and social struggles. Many are disenfranchised and have lost hope. What will you offer that will resurrect what has died, revive what is lying dormant, and blow a wind of change that is so desired by many? Let's consider the landscape.

Economics. There are certain economic factors that may influence your decisions, strategies, and even your successes. These factors may include needed funding or capital investment, changes in federal legislation governing small business loans, and many market fluctuations and permutations that will require you to periodically change business strategies. People consistently resist change so, therefore, the challenges that you will face will be both internal and external. Yet, you are tooled with what's needed to navigate yourself and others through difficult periods and rough terrains.

Partnerships and Collaborations. We live in a global society. The business landscape has changed, and this change presents both benefits and obstacles to your efforts to reach your goals. It doesn't matter what structure you choose—for-profit, not-for-profit, or community group—you need people. You can't do it all (or have it all). You will need to fill in gaps with partnerships and/or collaborations to quickly scale your work within your community, region, or country. Trust in and encourage partnerships within your organization as you will quickly realize that this is a cost-effective means of increasing your organization's visibility, promoting its brand, and increasing your professional network.

Technological Advancements. Navigating through economic constraints will likely require that you adopt technologies that will reduce costs, increase efficiencies, and support your goals of organizational effectiveness. Let technology do what it does and bring on people to fulfill the "human" functions. A healthy marriage of human resources and technology will spare you many headaches.

How well you pull that off will depend upon your appreciation of technology, willingness to stay abreast of advancements, and your commitment to lead those who follow you into perpetual learning for their and the organization's constant and continual growth.

All of this comes down to ***leadership.*** Countless books have been written on leadership styles and theories and, boast of success stories. Rather than focus on whether or not you're the "right" kind of leader, focus on being a good leader that others are committed to following. After all, you're not a leader if no one is following you. Of course, this brings us full circle to being a visionary, for the visionary leads in a manner that enables growth of the organization as well as its people. However, the larger aspect of being a leader is being able to influence others and their decisions concerning you and your organization and its mission.

Surveying the landscape will inform you of many more aspects of business than leadership, partnerships, technologies, and economics. The overarching question is how do you see each of these and how will you go about conveying what you perceive? Do you see them from a birds-eye perspective that informs your decisions and strategies? In a world of political correctness, norms, and deference to others' titles and authorities, your license to break rules, blur lines, and travel in a lane that is all your own is your outlook on life and the world. If you can dream it, then you can do it, but how well you do it depends on how you perceive your business landscape and how you communicate that perception to others.

Your Modus Operandi

Dictionary.com defines modus operandi as "a particular way or method of doing something, especially one that is characteristic or well-established." Most will simply say that it's your "M.O." to take a specific course of action, given a certain set of circumstances.

Past employers and organizations have likely benefited from your willingness to provide input regarding business processes, strategic plans, and various implementations over the years. No one successfully operates a business, leads an organization, or mobilizes a movement within a dry landscape. Success always requires the fresh watering of ideas and the wisdom to identify what needs to be challenged by an alternative thought. If this sounds like your modus operandi, you may have overlooked your own contribution and even failed to realize that you've brought an added value to your role. Whether you've done it knowingly or unknowingly makes little difference. My challenge to you is to shine a bright light on this particular skill set. Why? Because it flows freely from your outlook on life and the world.

Your outlook is, indeed, one of the best parts of who you are. Your unique outlook on life isn't a practice of looking at the world through rose-tinted glasses. It is your ability to have a vision of what life could be, should be, and would be if you are bold enough to answer a calling or pursue a dream. Even if you've taken the route of education and degrees, learning theories and applications can only compliment or supplement what comes naturally. Without an ability to look deeper than what's on the surface and beyond the immediate horizon, parchment paper will fall short of enabling you to land on higher ground when you leap.

Taking back your POWER requires that you reclaim your outlook. However, reclamation of your outlook doesn't mean withholding ideas from others. It largely means having the courage to pursue a vision that is all your own. Are you bold enough to make those steps and take those actions that will progress you toward the fulfillment of a dream, vision, or situation that only you can see? Do you have the fortitude to continue to build, when it makes no sense to anyone around you, simply because they are unable to see life in quite the same way that you do? This is a challenge that separates the leader from the led, but for those who are bold enough to make one step, then two, it promises to be a journey that is very much worthwhile.

Reflections and Next Steps

(Keep it honest and personal)

Are you a visionary? If so, what makes this true?

_____

_____

_____

_____

_____

_____

_____

_____

_____

_____

_____

_____

Reflections and Next Steps

(Keep it honest and personal)

What is your unique way of looking at the world? How does this translate to your current job?

_____

_____

_____

_____

_____

_____

_____

_____

_____

_____

_____

_____

_____

Reflections and Next Steps

(Keep it honest and personal)

How has your present or prior employer benefited from your outlook? How has your employment situation influenced your outlook?

___

___

___

___

___

___

___

___

___

___

___

___

___

___

Reflections and Next Steps

(Keep it honest and personal)

Do you understand the difference between power and authority? If so, how has your outlook empowered you in your present work situation?

_____

_____

_____

_____

_____

_____

_____

_____

_____

_____

_____

_____

_____

Quote in Context~

"Misfortune is a stepping stone for genius, the baptismal font of Christians, treasure for the skillful man, an abyss for the feeble." -Honore de Balzac

Taking back your POWER is a process wherein you reclaim the best parts of who you are: your purpose, outlook, wonder, energy, and resources. What you have to offer others will likely be directly related to or influenced by your life experiences—both good and bad. Your ability to transition experiences to service opportunities will depend upon your worldview and how you choose to see yourself and your life experiences. Even misfortune holds value within life; not only your life, but the lives of others as well. These are your life lessons and potential stepping stones leading to greatness. So, adjust your outlook on adversity, disappointment, pain, i.e. your life and its experiences, and show others how to rise and excel.

CHAPTER THREE

You Are Fearfully and Wonderfully Made

"You weren't an accident. You were deliberately planned." –Max Lucado

For a moment, I want you to consider where you spend most of your time. Whether it's a job, a volunteer opportunity, your local church or community center, or home; makes no difference. I want you to ponder this aspect of your life and what your role is within that environment. When I speak of leadership or being a leader, that word encompasses not only a skill set but abilities as well. Leaders rise to the top, even without titles, capture the respect of their peers, and cause others to gravitate to and around them. But what enables a leader to do that?

Consider what you lend to your environment naturally—be it positive or negative. If you're committed to be your authentic self, then your leadership style and abilities flows naturally from who you are and is demonstrated through various aspects of your skill set. That's textbook. When you consider the process of taking back your POWER and reclaiming the best parts of who you are, one of your most essential aspects of your presentation, service delivery, quality of service, and consistency is your personal brand. There are many individual components that work together to make you *you* authentically. However, your personal brand is what sets you apart as a wonder among men.

What is Your Personal Brand?

If you've assumed that I'm about to start discussing your logo, you are mistaken. While your logo does have its contribution to you or your organization's brand, there's quite a bit more to branding your organization than a catchy graphic. In fact, your ability to define your corporate brand is necessary if you intend to develop a marketing plan for the organization. Why? Because it is the brand that ultimately drives the type of consistent loyalty that your business, organization, agency, ministry, etc. requires from clients, partners, and donors. However, before you're able to effectively develop a corporate brand, you must first define your *personal* brand. After all, anything that you establish (business, organization) or create (products or services) is only an off-shoot of who you are as an individual (the visionary).

So, let's dig into what makes you a wonder among men. Your ability to cause others to gather around a cause or initiative even without a title or authority to do so, drive sales in an area that most find to be hard ground, be the man or woman who brings the fresh wind of change when environments grow stale, and be able to pull it off with consistent quality—this creates an expectation of what you bring to the table again and again. Your personal brand develops and maintains the perception that your employer, your church, your family, friends and enemies, and the public has regarding who you are as a person or professional as well as the way that you approach service delivery. This ultimately aids in quantifying good will within your personal valuation, and this is what makes you a desirable hire, volunteer, friend, confidante, and much-watched competitor.

When you see the Pepsi Cola logo, what thoughts and memories come to mind? It's simple enough; three swirls—blue, white, and red—against an entirely-white background. Even without the brand name Pepsi Cola, the visual image has the ability to foster an emotional response, based upon your experience with the product.

For a great number of people worldwide, the Pepsi Cola logo brings many positive memories to the surface; memories of a cold, sweating soft drink against the backdrop of a hot, humid day. There's the experience of the sweet soft drink passing over their tongue, and the crisp carbonation hitting the back of their throat as they swallow. It's not a one-time experience. The memory has been reinforced within their minds again and again with deliberate consistency enough to establish emotional attachment and response to both the logo and the product. On both a mental and emotional level, the logo represents all that the product is—good and bad—as well as the level of satisfaction that is expected to be had with each can, bottle, or glass that is consumed.

That visual recognition, mental recollection, and emotional response doesn't just happen because you like the way Pepsi Cola tastes. Each of those pieces come together within your mind and emotions, because marketing and branding professionals spent hundreds of millions of dollars to develop and launch a branding strategy to place behind a quality product. Does the money being spent on marketing and branding budgets make your mouth water for a Pepsi?

No, the taste and texture of the soft drink does that.

What the branding effort does is establish a consistent visual and message, so that when you see the logo or a sweaty can of Pepsi, your memory of your experience is recalled. The emotions that you felt as you enjoyed your beverage are attached to the memory; and you want to feel that way again.

Have you ever known someone who is bright and talented, and whatever you ask her for within her niche comes out top notch, clean, and professional, but somewhere within the overall delivery there's a flakiness that accompanies the work every time? How about the guy who gives you excellent work, but it's not what you requested; it's what he believes is best for you and your project? Have you met the woman who is an asset to any project, but her attention span is short and she's most excited about the project that promises the quickest financial return? How about the guy who's competent, but he can't get anything done by a deadline? Perhaps you've met the excellent speaker who can address many topics, but their outgoing personality that never allows him to meet a stranger causes professionalism to be compromised by becoming too familiar too quickly.

I've known each of these people and, if you've met them, you've likely come across them within your daily routines, the workplace, or within your circle of friends and associates. They become our go-to people for things that we need to get done, because of their proximity and availability. We accept the negatives that we consistently experience, because of our familiarity with who they are and *how* they are. What I have come to realize is that we are the buyers of their personal brand. With that being said, someone has become the buyer of your personal brand. Make no mistake, you do have a personal brand, even if you haven't fully defined it yet. Remember what I shared earlier:

> *"Your personal brand develops and maintains the perception that your employer and the public [have] regarding who you are as a person or professional as well as the way that you approach service delivery."*

I want to challenge you to identify what your personal brand is. What I do realize is that this can be a difficult exercise to complete with honesty and transparency, because our greatest reflection is oftentimes found in the eyes of another individual. In short, it helps to have input from someone who is willing to be honest regarding how he or she sees you. With or without that person, let's take a walk down a road of self-assessment.

What mental and emotional response does your name elicit within others? What is the perceived way you deliver your message or service? We're not looking for perfection. We're looking for consistency. We're not even looking to determine areas of opportunity specific to your brand. Stick a pin in that for a later project.

While you're completing the process of taking back your POWER, reclaiming your personal brand is largely becoming knowledgeable of the valuation that has been placed upon you by others. Are you proficient but flakey? Are you competent but can't meet a deadline? Does your commitment dissipate when a bigger payoff is presented by someone else? Are you the itinerant speaker who can't reign in your tongue? Remember, the sweaty Pepsi bottle elicits thirst, because it promises to deliver the same taste and feeling consistently. Now that people have tasted of your product or service, are they thirsty for more of you?

Some Kind of Wonderful

"Truth was never meant to make you comfortable, unless you stand in the middle of it with acceptance" (Shannon L. Alder). Being a wonder among men does not mean that you've got a special designation. What it does mean is that your particular brand, whether or not you've clearly identified it, is making a contribution to someone's success in a way that only you are able. Reclaim that wonder and then grow it by:

Being authentically you. You don't need to be the next Bill Gates, Oprah Winfrey, Steven Spielberg, or Billy Graham. Those positions have been taken and the roles fulfilled well. No one can be a better Oprah than Oprah, and no can be a better you than you. You already have a brand. Make sure that it's built around the real you and not an artificial person concocted to impress. This approach to personal branding requires that you act a certain way, dress a certain way, speak a certain way, and exhaust yourself by attempting to be someone or something that is artificial. Know your brand and ensure that it is reflected in everything you do and say and projected to the world, so everyone gets the same message about who you are and what you represent.

Make your voice heard. Even if public speaking is not your thing, you must be prepared to avail yourself of opportunities to communicate who you are, what you do, what you stand for, etc. You're looking to take ownership of a certain space in the world. It's time to open your mouth and proclaim just that. You've got knowledge (the reason why your name comes to the remembrance of others) and power (the reason you can gather followers, even if you don't have a leadership title). That's the place where you need to speak from; a place of knowledge and power. This will become a source of confidence. Even when some decide to criticize you, your knowledge and power will enable you to stand your ground.

Being a thought leader. No, I don't mean a *thoughtful* leader (at least not in in this case). An effective means of establishing your credibility within your space in the world is to release thought leadership articles. This is your opportunity to give back, as there are others who are looking to know what you know and follow you where you're going. Your research and practical knowledge are the foundation to your credibility; so, share it. Effective and consistent releases establish a foundation upon which you may monetize your knowledge through interviews and speaking engagements.

Supporting your brand through social media. Whether you like it or not, we live in a social media world, and it can be beneficial or detrimental to your brand and work. So, you'll want to take command of the narrative, imagery, and media information that's made available to the world. Articles and images are taken from one location and shared to many locations across the Internet, each day. Publishing your own website as well as maintaining profiles on Facebook, Instagram, Twitter, YouTube, and LinkedIn empowers your ability to control how you are depicted on the Net while you monitor what others are saying and writing. All Internet publications should be consistent and lend toward the building, maintenance, and communication of your personal brand, even down to the connections that you allow.

Perpetually learning. If you want to be a visionary, you must become knowledgeable. Before you can advance what's being done, you must become aware of the foundations supporting what's presently in place. Don't trust solely in any knowledge that you currently have, because things change daily, and what is considered best practice today may not be respected tomorrow. Knowledge is power and the person with the latest knowledge has the competitive advantage. So, become a person who is constantly learning, reading, soliciting feedback, and watching for industry change. This will thrust you into industry leadership and position you to be a trailblazer.

A psalmist wrote, "**I will praise thee; for I am fearfully *and* wonderfully made: marvellous *are* thy works; and *that* my soul knoweth right well**" (Psalm 139:14, KJV). You were designed by the greatest of engineers, deliberately and specifically for your work. As you put in the time to identify, define, develop, and communicate what sets you apart as a wonder among men—your personal brand—you will become increasingly aware of the importance of claiming it before starting on your journey. This is the juncture at which you transition your brand from someone else's vision to your own vision and work. Taking back your POWER is a process, but reclaiming your wonder requires self-assessment, honesty, and work!

Reflections and Next Steps

(Keep it honest and personal)

Have you considered your personal brand? If so, what is it?

_____

_____

_____

_____

_____

_____

_____

_____

_____

_____

_____

_____

Reflections and Next Steps

(Keep it honest and personal)

Do you believe that those who are closest to you would agree with your brand statement?

_____

_____

_____

_____

_____

_____

_____

_____

_____

_____

_____

_____

Reflections and Next Steps

(Keep it honest and personal)

What are the strengths and weaknesses of your personal brand?

_____

_____

_____

_____

_____

_____

_____

_____

_____

_____

_____

_____

_____

Reflections and Next Steps

(Keep it honest and personal)

What strategies might aid in improving the weaknesses of your personal brand? Are you able to pull these strategies off alone or will you require assistance?

_____

_____

_____

_____

_____

_____

_____

_____

_____

_____

_____

_____

Quote in Context~

"You weren't an accident. You were deliberately planned." –Max Lucado

Years ago, I was employed by an Ohio-based accounting firm. From time to time, one of the partners would jokingly refer to words or deeds of a staff person as a "career-limiting" decision or action. While he generally meant it in jest, those words have stuck with me over the years.

There are many people who choose to brand themselves as *accidents* or *illegitimate*, simply because of the circumstances that allowed them to be born. These self-imposed labels serve only to limit their greatness and expanse of achievement. There are even those who have opted to sub-consciously take on those labels and worse, because others have imposed them upon their psyche. For all intents and purposes, their willingness to wear these labels has become a career-limiting decision as they are worn like a brand. One can't walk in their purpose while standing firmly under the mental and emotional banner of being an accident; and one can't express their authentic and unique self as a leader within their world, when he secretly deems himself to be illegitimate.

Look around you. Nothing and no one that you see is there by happenstance. It was all foreknown and planned. Laying aside career-limiting labels will prove to be both liberating and empowering, but such an action requires self-evaluation and the willingness to embrace personal truths.

CHAPTER FOUR

When Life Becomes Little More Than a Time Suck

"Sometimes exhaustion is not a result of too much time spent on something, but of knowing that in its place, no time is spent on something else." -Joyce Rachelle

The Bible instructs leaders to **"write the vision, and make *it* plain upon tables, that he may run that reads it."** Countless books on organizational management have been written, and most of them rest soundly upon the importance of communicating vision. From time to time, there is a need to focus on the outcome of hearing the vision and the act of running.

It is a truth that there are many successful businesses, ministries, and organizations throughout the world. Therefore, it is safe to assume that there are many *runners* with varying levels of commitment to the cause and vision of the organization that employs them. So, I ask you this question. How much of your limited energy is being expended running after someone else's vision and dream? While you ponder that question, just know that life is always in a state of flux; and between the 9 to 5 job, taking care of others, taking care of yourself, juggling relationships, and squeezing in much-needed rest, you might become a bit drained. It's time to reclaim your *energy*!

Early in my career, I oftentimes found myself becoming burned out with the work I was doing, the company for which I was working, and even organizations where I volunteered my time. My remedy for burn out became change—change what I was doing or opt to do something routine but in a new environment or situation. This provided the illusion of being reenergized, at least temporarily. Over the years, the words "life is a teacher" became a maxim of mine; and those words proved true time and time again. So, give me a few minutes and I'll share what life has taught me.

Where's the Passion?

Burn out is more than just a catchy phrase. It's real. If you're experiencing chronic fatigue, lack of energy, loss of appetite, forgetfulness, depression, and anger, chances are that you're not just moody – you're burned out. Although I introduced this chapter referencing those who are working for someone, you don't have to be anyone's employee to experience burn out. It just seems that men and women who are within situations that are beyond their economic control tend to manifest these symptoms more. Just know that even self-employed individuals experience burn-out. So, back to what life has taught me. Burn out is oftentimes a symptom of a life that is absent passion; passion for the work that you do, for the cause that you represent, for the ministry that you serve, etc.

Is passion driving the work that you do? Consider this; are you waiting for a point in time when you'll receive *the big payout* for the work that you do and the contribution that you've made? It makes no difference if you're a software developer anticipating a $1 million payday or clerk looking forward to retiring from a $40,000 per year situation. If you are dreaming of *the big payout* more than the next accomplishment, you've likely lost the passion for your work.

Do you find yourself living for the weekend? On average, you'll work 8-10 hours each weekday. I'm a big supporter of living in the moment and appreciating what is being offered, addressing challenges head-on, and being present for those who need or rely upon you. If your entire disposition changes on Sunday afternoon, because you anticipate going to work on Monday morning, and Friday never seems to come soon enough—you've likely lost the passion for your work, if you ever had it at all.

Do you remember a time when you would become angry on the job—angry about the quality of the work, the service level rendered to customers, cutbacks in required areas, etc.? Are you noticing that you're no longer emotionally invested in what happens within the organization? Many may view emotional outbursts as negative, but oftentimes it's those moments that demonstrate the passion for the work, the cause, or the organization's mission. When you're no longer emotionally invested, and everything begins to slide off your back like a duck, you've likely lost the passion for the work that you do.

Do you remember a time when you would talk about your job or the projects within which you were involved? Consider that grandmother who carries a portfolio of photographs of that somewhat cute granddaughter or grandson in her wallet. It seems that as friends and strangers approach, she's grabbing that wallet to free those photos and engage in discussion—doesn't matter if the person is interested or not. You were like that grandmother, only you discussed your job, your supervisor, the annual fundraiser, new hires, and layoffs. The conversation was endless; but now, you don't talk about your job unless someone asks you first. Guess what? You've lost the passion for the work that you do.

What I've discovered is that, just as I was, many people go through the motions of living rather than tapping into something that motivates them, energizes them, and feeds a burning passion to do and be. It was only after I identified that *thing* that I was passionate about that the commitment that I placed behind it no longer drained me of my energy. Absent passion, you will be a person for hire, driven by necessity rather than a life-affirming reason to invest a significant amount of your time and talent to advance a thought, movement, or a work. In such a mental state, life becomes little more than a time suck as you sell 2,080 hours of your life, year after year until you qualify for retirement—then your real issue will become clearly pronounced, as you realize there isn't much point to getting out of bed each day, absent a defined purpose. When you lack passion, at some point, even breathing will seem to drain you of your energy.

Dare to Dream!

Boldly reclaiming your energy involves being honest enough to identify what is ultimately a waste of your time and outside of your purpose, and further being willing to set those things aside, despite relationships and circumstance, to pursue life-breathing purpose with genuine passion. Take a moment, right now, and dare to dream about what could be. If you could be and would be more, what would that more be? Consider this a safe place. For just a minute, forget about every financial barrier, every nay-saying voice, and every deep-seeded fear. Reclaiming your energy starts right here, in this moment. Past and future are irrelevant. You can't change the past; so, glean what you can from your experiences and move forward. You can't control the future; so, hope, faith, and a written plan are what you need to be prepared to unpack. Remember, **"write the vision, and make *it* plain upon tables, that he may run that readeth it."** The first person who must be willing to run with your vision is you!

Here's a story that should be included within every entrepreneurial training curriculum across the country. Cory Nieves was a six-year-old boy who, without any real ability to make a life-changing decision, declared that he was tired of catching the bus to school and wanted to buy a car. That declaration wasn't the idle chatter of a spoiled child attempting to obtain privilege or avoid inconvenience. It was the seed of personal motivation coming alive in the fertile soil of someone who was willing to do something he'd never done to have something he'd never had. It's likely fair enough to assume that Cory didn't know anything about business plans, profit and loss statements, or break-even analysis. What he did know was that life, in general, could be more than what it was.

Without venture capital backing or even a credit score, Cory began selling hot cocoa to the residents of Englewood, New Jersey. That later grew to lemonade and cookie sales to save money for college. It seems he hit pay dirt with the cookie idea. Today, Mr. Cory's Cookies offers a variety of flavors and taps into the less-occupied market of preservative-free snacks. Through hard work and the boldness to put action behind a dream, his Mr. Cory's Cookies has become an enterprise that has worked with major brands such as Pottery Barn, Barney's, Aetna, J. Crew, Citibank, Ralph Lauren, and Whole Foods, to name a few. All of this before his fourteenth birthday.

Allow me to introduce you to Jamie Brewer. Jamie is an actress, model, and activist. On the surface, that might strike one as being somewhat unremarkable, in today's society. However, what's an ever-present reality within her life and world is that she has Down's syndrome. Despite this disorder, Jamie has transitioned from being a theatrical actress to portraying attention-grabbing roles on prominent television shows, including *American Horror Story* and *Southland* and has been cast in movie roles as well. In a world of firsts, she owns the designation of being the first woman with Down's syndrome to be featured during New York's Fashion Week.

Jamie consistently demonstrates that there's more to her than learning lines and walking catwalks. She's served as President of the Arc (National Autism Resource & Information Center) of Fort Bend Chapter—the youngest person to ever be elected to the post. Thereafter, she was appointed to the State of Texas Arc Board, and further elected to the Executive Board in the capacity of the Treasurer. Serving as the Arc Governmental Affairs Committee for the State of Texas, she's been instrumental in persuading State legislators to pass laws abolishing the use of the "R" word and further advanced legislation that is positively impacting Texas residents with disabilities. While a vast majority might assume that her disability serves as a barrier to her being a productive member of society, her infectious energy won't allow that to be true.

The world has many change agents who are making a difference within their lives as well as within the lives of others. See, when I speak of boldly reclaiming your energy, I'm challenging you to grab firmly onto your ability to believe so deeply in an idea, a cause, a movement, a calling, or a dream, and run like crazy with it until you notice that others are running alongside and behind you. The boldness of the action is speaking the dream as though it's an intention, and then running before others fully understand what you're doing and why you're doing it.

Excuses are of little value and only serve to delay or deter you from who and what you can be. What excuses have you empowered to suppress you from achieving personal victories, successes, and legacies? Are you too young; or perhaps, too old? Do you not have enough money to do anything significant? Are you so stuck in a rut of planning that you never actually begin a work? Are you disabled? Have others placed labels and limitations upon you? Robert F. Kennedy once said, *"There are those that look at things the way they are, and ask why? I dream of things that never were, and ask why not?"* Looking over your life, what perspective have you chosen to have with most consistency—looking at the realities or dreaming of the possibilities?

Some of the greatest people in history were ordinary men and women (and even boys and girls) who had the ability to dream and were committed to sharing their dream with others. They were bold enough to exert their energy upon others—individuals, groups, crowds, and communities—until that energy created heat, and that heat ignited a burning fire of change; change within their own lives as well as the lives of others. We live in a society that celebrates the famous and feeds a social engine that perpetually rewards them just for being, showing up, and striving for relevance. The real greatness lies within the ordinary and the dreamers—the Cory's and the Jamie's and, yes, YOU!

What is your dream that continues to breathe during your waking hours? The progression from dream to reality requires that you exert the energy required to cause people to gather around a vision that is all your own. Taking back your POWER cannot happen effectively absent the energy to accomplish the desired work. Boldly reclaiming your energy is a necessity as your energy is what enables you to tap into your greatest of resources—people. My challenge to you today is that you will clearly define your vision, speak it out loud, and resolve to be the first of many who run after they've heard it.

Reflections and Next Steps

(Keep it honest and personal)

Do you have a vision for your business, organization, ministry, or cause? If so, what is it?

_____

_____

_____

_____

_____

_____

_____

_____

_____

_____

_____

_____

_____

_____

Reflections and Next Steps

(Keep it honest and personal)

Who have you shared your vision with? How do you go about sharing your vision?

_____

_____

_____

_____

_____

_____

_____

_____

_____

_____

_____

_____

_____

Reflections and Next Steps

(Keep it honest and personal)

Are you apprehensive about sharing your vision with others? What is greater at this time, your excitement to share your vision or the fear of what others will think after hearing it?

_____

_____

_____

_____

_____

_____

_____

_____

_____

_____

_____

_____

_____

Reflections and Next Steps

(Keep it honest and personal)

You want people to run after hearing your vision. Do you have a plan that will guide those who are running behind you?

_____

_____

_____

_____

_____

_____

_____

_____

_____

_____

_____

_____

_____

Quote in Context~

"Sometimes exhaustion is not a result of too much time spent on something, but of knowing that in its place, no time is spent on something else." -Joyce Rachelle

While people are your greatest business resource, time is your greatest personal resource. Like money, you can only spend it once. It's a limited resource; you're allotted 24 hours each day at most. The process of reclaiming your POWER won't be complete, if you fail to realize what you're allowing to absorb your time. Sometimes, the most severe case of burnout is due to a dreamer's time being absorbed and energy being exhausted while chasing another man's dream, selling another man's vision, and working to advance another man's agenda. These actions require a level of commitment that entangles both the time and resources of those who invest themselves to keep initiatives alive and active. Every moment spent to ensure the life of one initiative is a moment withheld from the life of another.

… … …

CHAPTER FIVE

This Thing Really Is a Give and Take

"When you believe in your dream and your vision, then it begins to attract its own resources. No one was born to be a failure." -Myles Munroe

We each have both strengths and weaknesses. It makes sense that we tend to focus on our strengths and do what is necessary to fortify the weak areas. Resource management is an area in which I've worked, in one respect or other, for over 30 years. As an accountant and financial manager, I've taken on the practice of quantifying *everything*. As peers pitched ideas for program development, I would mentally tick off the costs, e.g. additional hours (tick), equipment (tick), office space (tick), program consultant (tick). As the pitch went on, the budget got bigger, and I would prepare my impromptu response regarding how a commitment of limited resources requires fiscal offsets. To get a little, the program manager would need to give a little.

As you're progressing through your process of taking back your POWER, it seems only fitting that we round out the components with the R within our POWER acronym—Resources. I refer to my experience dealing with resource management, but the reality is that we all deal with managing resources; and we do it daily.

Consider this morning routine:

5:30 a.m.	Alarm sounds
6:00 a.m.	Time to shower and dress
7:00 a.m.	Play chemist with the preparation of coffee
7:20 a.m.	Grab the keys and run out of the house
8:00 a.m.	Arrive at work—respond to emails, answer calls and prep for meeting #1
9:00 a.m.	Meeting #1
11:00 a.m.	Respond to emails, address staff issues, and put out a fire
11:30 p.m.	Review budget for meeting #2
12:00 p.m.	Working lunch while completing report

Take it in and realize that although this is only the first 7 ½ hours of a worker's day, it is an experience and routine shared by many within our country. Consider the dozens of mindless decisions that were made before noon, e.g. hit the snooze button…and how many times? What to wear? Instant coffee or brewed? Will I stop for breakfast? What's for lunch? Risk highway traffic or take the back roads? Respond to emails now or later? Return phone calls now or later? Order in or go out for lunch? Working through lunch? What will I present at the meeting? In the midst of all of this, there is an expectation that creative juices will flow freely, ideas will be communicated, and that personal brand that your supervisor has come to rely upon will outshine every circumstance, emergency, and time constraint. Sometimes, it seems that the talented are those who are able to squeeze in productive work time between meetings to discuss productivity.

Now, consider your routine. Are you a program manager, an office administrator, customer service representation, secretary, etc.? I could cover the full gamut of employment classifications, but most will still render hectic schedules that routinely pull you away from the core elements of the work that you like to do. Somehow, you make it all work, and the way that you do that is by feeding an ever-burning furnace that takes on a look that is acceptable to each of us, i.e. a corporate position, a community program or agency, a charitable cause, a worthy mission, or even a family dynamic—feeding it with your resources.

When we talk about taking back your POWER and reclaiming your resources, it's important to note that resources are not just money. It's easy to focus on money, because it's quantifiable and tangible. You exchange money for goods and services, and you see the value of what you've gained in the exchange. You set money aside and you see the interest accumulate on its time value. So, yes, we'll discuss money but there are other resources that are greater than money—resources that you sell, give away, or take for granted daily.

Money, Time, and Energy

Money. Aside from what I've already mentioned about money, it is not to be regarded for more than what it is—a resource. It's been said that *"money is a fantastic servant but a brutal master."* Once one becomes knowledgeable of the four pillars of wealth, it is the easiest of your resources to manage. However, some might argue that it is the most difficult to obtain. From the standpoint of reclaiming your resources, money is the easiest to envision, because its reclamation oftentimes involves redirecting your spending from one place to another, e.g. redirecting funds from a charitable organization that you support to another that you've founded.

Another aspect of the process is having and maintaining a healthy relationship with money and further respecting the sources of additional money. What do I mean by respecting the sources? If you want to accumulate money, it should be noted that financial gains can only come from another person, i.e. a customer, an employer, or profits of an investment. Because the source of monies is ultimately someone other than yourself, it is just good business sense and practice to respect those who are present or potential revenue sources.

Time. The perception of time as a resource is largely due to it being a constant. Everyone receives up to 24 hours each day. It is never increased. In fact, when you consider that a day of death is imminent as early as one's day of birth, between the points of birth and death is a span of time. Because there is only so much available and allocated, and the amount of time one has is an unknown, it becomes one of the most valuable of your resources. When you look at time as a limited resource of unknown quantity, then you'll come to realize that you can't afford to waste it, and you certainly won't allow others to waste it for you.

Reclaiming your time as a resource involves making a daily determination regarding what's important, making a commitment to handle important items now, and then ensuring that there is organization driving your approaches and methods to getting things completed. You not only want to be effective in your work, you want to be efficient in the manner that it's handled.

Energy. I dedicated the whole of chapter four to discussing energy. So, I won't spend a lot of time on it here. However, it should be noted as a takeaway that energy as a resource is referenced from the perspective of the amount of effort that is invested into an activity. Energy is purely subjective and difficult to measure. Reclaiming it as a resource speaks to redirecting these efforts from another man's work to the work or project to which you are committing your time.

It's arguable that anything that's measured is improved upon. This is true when you consider your money, energy, and time. These are three of the resources that you have likely sold, given away, or taken for granted. These are also aspects of who you are that others are consistently prepared to take, receive, or consume for their own benefit as well as that of the organization, mission, or work that they represent. Reclaiming these resources will largely require that you become equally informed regarding the value of your contribution—the contribution of your resources.

If you want to strike out on your own, you will need resources. If you want to initiate personal and professional development within your life, you will need resources. If you want to transition your dreams to reality, you will need resources. When you invest these resources properly, there will be a return that will empower you to accrue assets, fund your work and projects, and independently pursue the calling that is specific to you and your life. However, before we move on, there is a fourth resource that is arguably the most important.

You Are the Resource

Reclaiming your resources is not driven by an act to withhold your time, energy, or money from another viable business. The greater reality within this process is that you are the resource. All of the talent, skill set, and knowledge that walks through the door with you each day—that is the resource that is drawn from with regularity. If an organization, church, agency, or community outreach has you, then it has your time, energy, and money as well. As you contemplate making a move to start that business, nonprofit, or community service of your own, you will launch in a manner that is handicapped, if you fail to reclaim your resources by redirecting your commitments.

Taking back your POWER is first an acknowledgement that you are not power*less*. It's a realization that you've been tooled for success. Just ask those who have succeeded because of your labors. There's a time and season for everything. If you believe that this is your time, and this is your season to become an entrepreneur, community leader, business owner, etc., then the challenge that is being presented to you is to boldly reclaim your resources and resolve to make that first empowered step toward your personal destiny.

Reflections and Next Steps

(Keep it honest and personal)

What resources do you have to help fund your own business or organization?

_____

_____

_____

_____

_____

_____

_____

_____

_____

_____

_____

_____

Reflections and Next Steps

(Keep it honest and personal)

What resources, if any, are you selling, giving away, or taking for granted daily? Who or what is benefiting?

_____

_____

_____

_____

_____

_____

_____

_____

_____

_____

_____

Reflections and Next Steps

(Keep it honest and personal)

What do you believe will be the consequence of redirecting your resources to your new business endeavors? Are you concerned about this consequence? Why?

___

___

___

___

___

___

___

___

___

___

___

___

Reflections and Next Steps

(Keep it honest and personal)

What is the monetary value of the time that you give to others? What is the basis of your valuation?

_____

_____

_____

_____

_____

_____

_____

_____

_____

_____

_____

_____

Quote in Context~

"When you believe in your dream and your vision, then it begins to attract its own resources. No one was born to be a failure." -Myles Munroe

Belief in one's dream is a requirement. The dreamer must be the greatest believer. But it takes much more than belief to realize a dream and further become a leader of those who would follow a vision. To gain momentum and see progress, one must have resources. So, what is the connection between vision and resources? Your passion for the work drives one to share an awesome vision. It is the vision that compels others to gather around and freely contribute their time, talents, skill sets, and money. No one was born to be a failure. However, when one fails to allow their passion to breathe, the world is deprived of an opportunity to be invested in something great.

CHAPTER SIX

POWER Up!

"You do have a story inside you; it lies articulate and waiting to be written behind your silence and your suffering." -Ann Rice

I stated early on that this book isn't meant for everyone, and it's at this point that you have an opportunity to decide if it is, indeed, meant for you. Reclaiming your POWER is a necessity for your success as a business owner and as an effective leader. This is a truth; and by now, I expect that the truths that I've shared have awakened dormant dreams, caused you to remember who and what you are meant to be, and have planted a seed of change deep within your mind and thoughts. So, what's next? Now that you've read about the five aspects of POWER, how do you go about applying it to your life and realities in a practical and sustainable manner? It takes more than being inspired. Before you get caught up in the moment and zealously chase the dream, let's slow it down and activate what's been learned. It's time to POWER Up!

Let's consider this…the definition of the term *power up* is "to cause to operate"[1]. That's exactly the mindset and action that we're going for. By the time you finish this book, I want you to be well

---

[1] https://www.merriam-webster.com/dictionary/power%20up

beyond being inspired, prepared to step into leadership, and actively making strides to operate in your purpose—activating the dream that's meant to live vibrantly during your waking hours. POWERing Up is your activation for operation within your purpose. So, let's take time to take another look at your POWER from a different perspective.

The Lost and Found | Purpose

When I was in grade school, there was a box in the principal's office that contained random gloves, jackets, hats, shoes, etc. waiting to be claimed. That box was *the lost and found*. After preoccupied children dropped or misplaced items, they were collected and placed in the lost and found to give the child both time and opportunity to realize that they've lost something of value, name it, and further take action to request its return. In many instances, the request is never presented, because the lost items are oftentimes replaced by other items as it is decided that expending the time, energy, and resources to obtain another set of gloves, another jacket, or another pair of shoes is preferred over presenting their humanity before a person of authority, admit that they've lost something, and be directed to the box of lost items to peruse and retrieve their property. After all, some of the items in the lost and found weren't actually lost. They were the gloves that a grandmother gave as a Christmas gift, but they looked like Grandma picked them out; or they weren't the right pair of shoes, so they were *lost* to present a legitimate need for replacement items to their parents.

What I've learned as an adult is that the lost and found is not just a childhood concept. It lives and persists within society. Local business offices, metro stations, restaurants, amusement parks—all of these maintain a lost and found that collect wallets, purses, jewelry, cell phones, clothing, etc. All these things, just like the lost and found in my grade school, are just waiting for someone to declare that they've lost something of value, name it, and pursue its return. Another reality about the lost and found is that, from time to time, others who have an immediate need are directed to the lost and found to chance finding something that will provide a momentary relief. Have you ever seen someone emerge wearing something that is ill-fitting or contrary to who and what they are? That's because their need has caused them to wear someone else's value. So, they walk away with someone else's unclaimed item because as ill-fitting as it may be, it's serving a purpose within that individual's life.

So, why am I spending time on the lost and found? Because many people forfeit their purpose to the lost and found. It's left discarded on the floor at their place of employment, misplaced at their local church, forgotten within their home or their community work. It has lost none of its value, even as it awaits the owner or *someone* to claim it. It's disregarded, because of their immaturity or it's discarded, because it doesn't look quite the way that they desire.

Many people who fail to walk in their purpose simply claim that they don't know what their purpose is. What is more often the reality is that the experiences that were designed to prepare them to give birth to purpose are rejected. These experiences are labor pains that lead to a dull, aching, stretching that effectively prepares one for the birth of something greater than who and what he or she is. Because the pain isn't appreciated, it and all that would come from it are rejected. The prayers go up to be led to their purpose as though a new purpose will be fashioned to replace what was forfeited to their personal lost and found.

It's been said that "your misery becomes your ministry", because it's the challenges that we face and overcome in life that prepare us to recognize needs within society, identify gaps in services, and effect needed change that positively impacts the lives of others. When one reflects on their experiences with shame, embarrassment, anger, and resentment rather than discerning their value, therein lies the impetus to bury these life-changing events and, by doing so, leave them on the floor of their life and routines; and they become a part of life's lost and found. So, others borrow from our life story and experiences to meet their needs, even when what they've borrowed is ill-fitting. They use them, because they recognize the value of what's been *lost* and waiting to be claimed.

He who learns must suffer. And even in our sleep pain that cannot forget falls drop by drop upon the heart, and in our own despair, against our will, comes wisdom to us by the awful grace of God. ~Aeschylus

Practical steps to knowing purpose, walking in purpose, and reclaiming purpose include being able to take possession of your experience. After all, it's your experience that qualifies you to be a leader in your area of knowledge and expertise. It's your experience that has shaped your past, influenced your decisions, informed your future, and equips you with a testimony of right and wrong. It's time out for fear, shame, and regret when it comes to the things of the past. The unabated momentum of qualified leadership comes at a high cost of authenticity, transparency, and revisiting *a pain that cannot forget* for the sake of advancing others through a familiar terrain and landscape, whether it's within business, faith, service, or life in general.

The second, practical step that I would offer is to take on a resolve to fight for your purpose. There are many challenges that we face daily, such as issues with family, employers and co-workers. Those are normal challenges, however irritating or frustrating they may be. When one adds in health issues, financial hurdles, and relationship conflicts, the overarching challenge that's set before us is maintaining sufficient focus to continually and consistently forge ahead with personal development, business establishment, and celebration of private victories that reframe narratives within our lives.

Internal and external opposition would cause one to become both distracted and discouraged from pursuing those things that others might define as *dreams* and long-shot opportunities. It's important to know that what you perceive as your purpose might well be viewed as a waste of your time as well as a waste of the time that others might lend to hear what you have to offer. It's not the job of nay-sayers to believe in you or your purpose. That's your job. Being resolved to fight means pressing past the thoughts and opinions of others as well as internal doubts and insecurities that would cause you to pause when you should move full steam ahead. If you're going to be a leader in a field of work, in your community, in your local church, or even in your home, then leading others starts with your own movement;

taking one step, then two. You can't win a game by being a spectator in the stands. You've got to get in the game and fight for your victory.

A World of Solutions | *Outlook*

I want to challenge you to see the world differently. Being an effective leader requires that you have an elevated point of view; consistently looking at life and circumstances from a higher perspective and with a wider lens. In other words, you need a sense of the bigger picture. Otherwise, you (and those who follow you) risk getting stuck in the weeds of circumstances, life, and business. Consider the trope "find a need, meet a need." It is the foundation of successful business and the framework of effective leadership.

Weeds, insects, sickness, disparity, inconvenience, unhappiness, etc. all are but a very few of the infinite realities of everyday life and day to day routines for many people within society. If you think for a few moments, you might be able to easily add to this list with problems witnessed or experienced within your family, neighborhood, state or region. Life generously offers challenges, but your ability to imagine solutions is your personal thoroughfare to success and effective leadership. A sense of the bigger picture allows you to acknowledge problems but reframe them as opportunities. When you become proficient in this practice, your body may exist in a world and society full of problems, but your mind will live in a world full of solutions.

In my book *Sometimes, Man's Rejection Is God's Protection*, I discuss the purpose and importance of the chief cornerstone. With that in mind, let's consider the curious bystander observing stonework at a local quarry:

A curious bystander observed four stonecutters working diligently in a local quarry. Driven by nothing more than his own nosiness, he approached each of the workers who were each in their own worlds cutting blocks of stone. Approaching the first stonecutter, he asked him what he was doing. "Just doing my job, sir," was the worker's quick answer. Dissatisfied with the response, the bystander moved on to the second stonecutter and asked the same question. "I'm cutting a stone!" The ambiguous response only encouraged the bystander to press on to the third stonecutter and ask him what he was doing. "I am cutting a stone to meet building specs; the right shape, size and density to bear weight." With much more understanding, he approached the final stonecutter. With great enthusiasm, the stonecutter stepped away from his work to greet the curious gentleman who asked the worker what he was doing. His reply was brief but packed with purpose. "I am building a place of worship."

Do you see yourself in the responses of any of the stonecutters? The story of the curious bystander speaks to perspective and vision. Each of the stonecutters has the same title, job function, and assignment. The first stonecutter has no vision. He is simply a worker being paid to complete a job. The second performs, but does so without thought; so, he performs the work by rote. The third stonecutter demonstrates attention to detail and a skill set to ensure the perfection of the product, but he is only carrying out some else's instruction. However, it is the fourth worker who sees the bigger picture driving the work that he's doing. He is the most enthusiastic; his enthusiasm being fed by an awareness that he is meeting a need within his community—the bigger picture. Whether you want to build a business, a place of worship, a movement, or a life in general, you will be best served by being able to see life and circumstances from a birds-eye view, taking in all aspects of challenges set before you, and making informed decisions that are not fettered by norms, opinions, or fears.

I want to offer two practical steps to adopting a big-picture view of life and effectively translating that to your dreams, visions, and work of leading others. The first step is to stock a mental toolkit with a series of questions that you can use to evaluate personal and business challenges as they arise. Those questions may include:

- How big is the problem, really?
- In the long-run (three to five years), how big will this problem seem?
- How much of this problem is real, and how much of it is fear?

- Assuming that this is an opportunity disguised as a problem, how must I look at it to completely reframe it in my mind and thinking?
- What can I realistically do, and what barriers are between me and that (actionable) decision?

Questions such as these aid in elevating your thinking above and beyond problems and frees your mental eye to see solutions. Your mental toolkit must be personal and specific to you. It is your resource to draw from rather than a cache of emotions that may mislead or cause you to be anchored to situations and constantly tethered to people, circumstances, fears, and anxieties that make it difficult to see anything beyond the smoke that they create.

The second, practical step that I would like to offer is that you develop a strategy to accompany your big-picture thinking. After all, being a person who sees a world of solutions has little value if you have no strategic plan to progress yourself and others toward any of them. In the context of leadership, strategy is your roadmap guiding you toward what you want to achieve.

It is important to note that your ability to be a leader is not founded upon your title or job function. Whether you are the CEO of a company or the janitor who empties the CEO's trash at end of the day, you will be measured by the impact you've had on others through your leadership as well as how that leadership has positively influenced the work and lives of those who have encountered you and your vision.

According to John Maxwell, "A leader's lasting value is measured by succession." In leadership, it's not about you. It's about those who trust in you, your knowledge, and abilities enough to follow you. They are your greatest resource and are your leadership legacy. Led well, people will continue to work toward your vision long after you're gone. You just need to make sure that your vision is big enough to accommodate the future, and then instill in your followers the ability to view life, markets, and the world in a manner that constantly turns the soil of their environment for repeated planting and harvests.

You've Got a Way About Yourself | Wonder

Here's an interesting statistic: The world's population is about 7.7 billion people, and it's growing at a rate of roughly 82 million people each year. If we're all fearfully and wonderfully made, then that's a lot of wonder gracing the planet. Consider this constantly-growing population. Who would you compare yourself to? I know that seems like a strange question to ask, but it's a pertinent place to be for now. Are you comparing yourself to friends and family? How about that celebrity who's dominating the media cycles right now? How about your former self? Think about it.

For many, this is a big problem: we want to step into a personal greatness by exercising that *thing* that is unique to us, but we compare ourselves to family, friends, icons, and even our former selves. Doing so only communicates a desire to be measured and defined by standards associated with those whom we've come to admire. Let's consider, for a moment, people who build and maintain their identity based upon past achievements. This is also very common, because it's natural to take pride in one's accomplishments. The downfall in this practice is that one can become locked within a pattern of comparing their potential to their past. If either of these life patterns sounds like yours, my challenge to you today is simple. Stop it!

You'll never become a profound expression of what makes you unique if you opt to dwell within the safety of being like others or become stuck in your own personal time loop, constantly revisiting a past that's losing value to who you are today. Dwelling on past accomplishments can be just as crippling as dwelling on past failures. The truth is that your decision to take back your POWER is driven by a realization and knowing that there is more for you—more to have, more to give, and more achievement within a different vein. You've got a way about yourself that makes you unique among 7.7 billion people. Tap into it. Exploit it. Herald its value from the highest rooftops.

Earlier, I shared insights concerning your personal brand. When I reference stepping into a personal greatness by exercising that *thing* that is unique to who you are, I'm referencing your personal brand;

not just your talent, or your gifting, or your skill set, but the way that you bring it all together by a governing work ethic to provide a product or service to society. When it's done well, a personal greatness has the potential of becoming national or international greatness.[2] Growing that brand into an intangible support for a thriving business takes time and patience, commitment, and consistency.

> *Time and Patience.* Building a business, an organization, or a movement that positively impacts people for years to come rarely happens overnight. When I began to engage others as a business consultant, it took time for me to perfect both my process and my interaction with companies and organizations. When I began supervising and managing others, there were lessons yet to be learned that were not covered in textbooks and even the best of business publications. More than business opportunities, these were learning opportunities that aided in my own professional development. Mistakes were made. Judgement calls weren't always the best. Life is a teacher, and if you want to learn, you've got to show up for class and live!
>
> It has been my experience that anything of value takes time, whether it's personal development, honing a craft, building a relationship, launching a business initiative, or developing a personal brand. Nothing of real value comes easily. Real entrepreneurs come to know this truth all too well, but the space that exists between their present realities and a future vision of how things

---

[2] Your personal brand cannot stand alone and flourish. It works hand in hand with your commitment to boldly walk in your purpose as well as your possession of a world and market view that is both deep and wide.

can be, should be, and will be is generally full of hunger, drive, and impatience. There's a certain hustle that accompanies entrepreneurism, and the transition from side hustle to viable business where one actually hires and/or leads others oftentimes requires a "ready, set, fire!" response to business opportunities. Absent an ability to take on patience, the continued use of this approach to business and its opportunities will cause you to operate in a valley of mistakes and bad judgement calls, and your reputation will suffer. If this is your experience, your personal brand may be repaired, but guess what it will require…time and patience.

Commitment. I want to offer three commitments that may help you. First, your commitment to yourself and others should be the daily manifestation of your best self, whatever the circumstance. That *best self* part encompasses many things. It includes your world view, your faith, your intellect, your knowledge, your skill set, your talents, and your character. Each are important and can influence or impact your brand.

> *Your personal brand is what people say about you when you are not in the room – remember that. And more importantly, let's discover why!* -Chris Ducker

Your personal brand is that certain something that causes people to call your number or pull up your website when a need enters their life or routine. It has little to do with your self-image or self-perception. In this instance, it's not about *self* anything; it's all about everyone else and how they view you. If your circle believes that you are the best thing since sliced bread, then it will make nothing but sense to them when you announce that you're stepping out on your own. You should expect and prepare for the referrals to start coming in. These may well be your foundational clients. Your employer, after grieving your resignation, may inquire about you becoming a contractor in some respect.

However, if your circle of friends, family, and associates think well of you but would not and will not refer you or the service that you provide to others, then there's a problem, and that problem is likely with your personal brand. So, the second commitment that I want to offer is your commitment to assess what others think, believe, and communicate about you and why they have those opinions. This should be done before you scale the work that you're doing or before you launch your business initiative before a larger audience. If you're able to acquire the honest opinions of five to 10 friends, family members, and associates and further recognize overlap among those opinions, then you've likely identified the strengths and weaknesses within your personal brand.

The third commitment that I will offer will aid you in your efforts to fortify the weaker areas of your personal brand: be committed to change. If people say that you're always late, then be committed to being on time. If people are not confident in your follow-through, then build into your business process communication and actions that close the loop. It's a truth that the likelihood of success in any business venture is directly related to how well the business knows its customer. This includes knowing what your customer knows (and thinks) about you.

Consistency. Being a profound expression of what makes you unique sounds wonderful, indeed. However, it only works to your advantage if you're able to do it consistently. When people entrust you with their talent, time, and resources, they are expecting that the same level of expertise and professionalism that drew them in will be there to meet their need time and time again. This expectation is had by both your customers and the people who you lead. Your ability to sustain the original impression that you make on others is supported by the authenticity of your brand. If you're being your authentic self, then it's not difficult to be consistent. Your actions, decisions, and service become expressions of who you are and what you have to offer.

A good name is more desirable than great riches; to be esteemed is better than silver or gold (Proverbs 22:1, NIV). The establishment of a credible personal brand is an action that's worthy of your time. The maintenance of that brand should take priority over all business initiatives. If scaling your business will compromise your ability to perform on a level that meets customers' expectations, then scaling the work isn't a good business move. When people patronize you, whether through your side hustle or through your national enterprise, they are purchasing your brand—your profound expression of what makes you unique. Remember, in a population of billions, you've got a way about you that sets you apart. The question is, will the way you do things encourage customers to dial your number when they have a need?

One-Quarter Tank of Gas | Energy

Are you at a point in your life where you're thinking of trading in your job for a career? Or perhaps, your career for a business? Do you feel like you've paid your dues, and you've absorbed all of the knowledge that you can from your present leadership? Has your mentor taken you as far as he or she can? Have you begun to formulate a plan to transition from your present reality to your dream? These are important questions; pertinent to where you are in life and the work that you do. Your answers will determine your resolve to pursue that dream that lives during your waking hours. What's equally as important as your resolve is your ability to take others with you as you embark upon what will certainly be a journey. Establishing a viable business initiative requires vision and people: customers, suppliers and workers. Gathering people around your vision requires energy. So, let's take a few moments to delve into your vision, before we touch on your energy again.

Remember, your transition from employee to business owner to employer will take time. This is a marathon, not a sprint. If you want your dream, organization, or movement to not only survive, but thrive, you will need to exert an energy that compels others to gather around your vision. That may sound somewhat ambiguous, so let's explore practical steps to creating that vision that will compel others to join your marathon and keep pace with your efforts to reach your specific goals. Your vision should be:

All about the people. If you want people to be compelled to chase after your vision, make sure that it begins and ends with people in mind. Long-term success lies in your commitment to believe, adopt, and act upon a mindset that it's not about your own advancement. It's about advancing a work that will change the lives of others. That means that you need to craft a vision that is externally-focused rather than internally-focused and driven by personal agendas. Your selfless vision will resonate with those who are of like mind and desire and compel them to join your ranks.

Clear and defined. A thriving organization oftentimes requires multiple talents and skill sets, e.g. accountants, managers, skilled workers, techies, and communications specialists, just to name a few. Your vision must be crafted in such a way that it not only enables but empowers people from varying walks of life and experiences to gather around it and gain commonality and agreement. This will be the foundation of your organization or movement's culture. Therefore, it needs to be as clear as possible. Ambiguity is not allowed. It must contain enough width and depth to capture the true scope of the venture and its impact upon and within the world, but at the same time be simple, easily understood, and able to fit within the minds of those people you need to make it a success.

Broadly articulated. Remember, there's a difference between your vision and your mission. Your vision may be to see a world without hunger, but your mission may be to develop an appropriate response to hunger among children 0-14 years of age by 2020. Your vision should address a real need and apply a perfect-world perspective of how it could be or should be. So, in this respect, take the gloves off and reach as high and as far as you can. Will you solve world hunger by 2020? Absolutely not. How about by 2040? Considering technology and agricultural advancements, who knows? But between now and then, your vision should be a motivator to constantly and consistently push toward advancement, improvement, and growth. You may outgrow your mission but outgrowing your vision should be very difficult if not impossible.

Measurable. No one wants to work tirelessly without seeing any results. That means that your vision needs to be measurable. A measurable vision statement allows for specific milestones that inform you and those who follow you how well you're doing. Whether you're making a short or long-term assessment, being able to look at concrete measurables will serve as an indicator of your progress and effectiveness.

Achievable in time. This is not an exercise in dreaming the impossible dream. However big your vision may be, it should not exceed your present and future resources required to make it happen, e.g. time, knowledge, finances, people, etc. Remember, the goal is to create a vision that will compel others to gather around it and take it on, so it should be reflective of your passion; but if you want it to have a needed credibility, it should also be reflective of your core competencies.

When I was in my 20's, I was reputed for driving, without worry, with less than a quarter of a tank of gas; a reputation that stayed with me into my 30's. Looking back on it, I couldn't tell you with great accuracy why I did it, other than it wasn't something about which I had great concern. I remember a friend of mine from college scolding me about this practice, and he warned that if I allowed my car to rest with less than a quarter tank of gas, my fuel line would likely freeze when the winter temperatures dipped during the night. I had no worries about the consequences, until consequence was upon me.

One morning, I had things all planned: prep for work, stop for gas, stop for breakfast, hit the highway, and get to work by 8:15. Things didn't work out that way, because I ran out of gas before I made it to the local gas station. As I sat on the side of the road, I experienced several epiphanies:

1. Those things that fuel your life and drive for achievement and continual progression should be kept in abundance;
2. Tomorrow isn't promised, but in case it comes, it should be met with a plan; and
3. A smart man learns from his mistakes, while a wise man learns from another man's mistakes.

Many who are driven to launch out on their own, do so with an inequity between their understanding of their drive and their energy to make it happen. So, in many respects, they are like my 20-something persona, driving pointedly with a quarter tank of gas. Dividing your message to people to accommodate where you are as well as where you want to be will cause you to burn your fuel all the quicker. At some point in time, you will need to decide whose vision you will push into the ears of your hearers. When you've decided that your purpose has taken on a voice that is louder than that of your employer, mentor, family, and friends, you will need to **write the vision, and make it plain upon tables, that he may run that reads it** (Habakkuk 2:2). Why? Because you will need people to start running excitedly for your vision with the same vigor and commitment that you've shown to others' vision. It's important to note that people gather to run behind leaders who are already running. Why should anyone follow you, if all you're doing is standing around waiting for followers? Is it even possible to follow someone who is standing still? Get to work!

Your energy enables you to influence others to run with you, contributing their time, talent, skill sets, and money. So, it's important that you don't end up on a side road of your life and experience, out of gas and reflecting upon your judgement calls. Consider my three *epiphanies*:

- Those things that fuel your life and drive for achievement and continual progression should be kept in abundance. If you don't want to run low on gas (energy), make sure there is a continual refueling occurring in your life. This happens when you surround yourself with people who believe, in word and deed, in you and your dreams.
- Tomorrow isn't promised, but in case it comes, it should be met with a plan. Life doesn't just happen. It is desired and worked. When you coast through life without regard to the consequences of failing to plan and further failing to act, life will become inconvenient and costly. If you want to be a leader, you must first learn to be a planner.
- A smart man learns from his mistakes, while a wise man learns from another man's mistakes. This one is most important. Don't reside in the "show me state." Be open to hear of the experiences and failures of others and learn how to avoid the pitfalls of business ownership, managing people, managing life, and scaling a work. If your mentor, employer, and family members have stumbled along the way, there's no need for you to stumble in the same way that they did. Learn from <u>their</u> mistakes!

Burning the Candle At Both Ends | Resources

When you consider your purpose and the demands that professional development places upon you to activate it within your life, it becomes quite necessary to recognize those people, actions, and commitments within your life that exhausts your resources. Remember, "boldly reclaiming your energy involves being honest enough to identify what is ultimately a waste of your time and outside of your purpose, and further being willing to set those things aside, despite relationships and circumstance, to pursue life-breathing purpose with genuine passion."

Now, consider your resources. Do they reflect your passions? Or do your passions reflect your resources? Does one have anything to do with the other? Think about it. You're likely familiar with the saying "burning the candle on both ends," and may have even used it at some point in life. For a few moments, let's delve into the meaning of the saying and see if it may have a practical application within your life.

Prior to Thomas Edison and Joseph Swan inventing filament light bulbs, people were greatly dependent upon candles to provide lighting. Such a need made candles very valuable and its users cognizant of the need to conserve as much as possible. So, in the 1700s, when people spoke of burning a candle at both ends, they referred to both ends of the candle being lit simultaneously. This would only be possible if the candle was held horizontally, lit on both ends and allowed to burn at twice the rate of normal usage. Considering the value of candles at the time, this idiom suggests wanton and reckless waste and poor judgement by the user. Consider the poem *Figs From Thistle: First Fig*, by Edna St. Vincent Millay[3]:

> My candle burns at both ends;
> It will not last the night;
> But ah, my foes, and oh, my friends—
> It gives a lovely light!

---

[3] Ref.: https://www.poetryfoundation.org/poetrymagazine/poems/14095/first-fig

Certainly, Millay communicates a willful abandon to consume her resources and does so recognizing the repercussions of her actions. She addresses both her friends and enemies to proclaim the pleasure of her decided waste. She experiences a light that will likely burn brightest at the last moment of its consumption. Now, if all of that makes sense, let's change the perspective up a bit. What if she's not referencing her resources, but her passion; and this last night is ablaze with eroticism? Does the poem take on an entirely different meaning, or may the two perspectives become reflective of the same reality concerning the moment's priorities?

When we talk about POWERing up, we're talking about effectively pulling each of the five components together in a manner that positions you to excel, lead, and prosper. Your purpose is overarching—an internal driver that compels an external work and outcome. Your outlook is your ability to see both the forest and the trees; enabling you to lead others through the rough terrains ahead. Your wonder is your unique and personal brand that expresses itself in a manner that causes others to trust who you are and what you have to offer. Your energy gives you the stamina to run with a determined vision and a visible excitement that draws followers. Your resources are your time, money, and mental and emotional resolve that you have available to invest according to your commitments. But where does passion fit in all of this? And how have you reconciled your passions with your current priorities?

Passion is the glue that holds all of this together; passion for the purpose, passion for the work, and passion for the future vision. When the passion dies, the work will die. If you fail to ignite a passion for whatever it is that you say that you desire or that work that you say you're purposed to accomplish, it will be nothing more than talk. Alongside the road of who and what you are right now and who and what you intend to be, there are signs to let you know that your resolve has you headed in the right direction. One of those signs is how you choose to consume your limited resources.

When you can clearly tie the consumption of your limited resources to your passion for the purpose, your passion for the work, and your passion for a future vision, then you will know with certainty that you've reclaimed this aspect of who you are. Over the years, one bit of counsel that I've shared with single female friends of mine who desire to be in a relationship: you will know that he's into you, when you are the recipient of his time and money. A man whose heart has been captured doesn't have a problem redirecting his resources to demonstrate how he feels. The same rings true when it comes to your resolve to leave a safe place and start something of your own. Allow your resources to evidence what your true passions and priorities are.

Do you have a dream that persists during your waking hours? Do you have mental notes, written notes, and pieces of the puzzle all around you? Is there an excitement within you that's comparable to an unexplainable pain, because you're aching to get started? Do you have a vision of a future that, at times, seems clearer than your present reality? If so, you sound like an entrepreneur who's ready to take the lead. I challenge you to revisit the five components of your POWER and truly assess if you've got enough passion—not excitement—to drive your own business initiative. Then you will know if you've effectively POWERed up!

Reflections and Next Steps

(Keep it honest and personal)

Consider your life and your greatest challenges and experiences? Have you taken ownership of these experiences in a way that empowers you?

_____

_____

Name three events or aspects of your life that have brought you your greatest happiness. What about these events or aspects of who you are bring you happiness?

_____

_____

Name three events or aspects of your life that have brought you your greatest sadness or despair? Are any of these aspects of your life recurring events?

_____

_____

Of the events and aspects of your life that you've named, which ones would change who you are significantly, had they never occurred?

_____

_____

Reflections and Next Steps

(Keep it honest and personal)

What need have you purposed to meet or resolve? Have you penned a three and five-year strategy for the work?

_____

_____

What do you have to offer that isn't already being marketed?

_____

_____

What is your personal brand? Write your brand statement. What are its strengths and weaknesses?

_____

_____

In what areas does your personal brand statement overlap with your family, friends, and customers' description of your personal brand?

_____

_____

Reflections and Next Steps
(Keep it honest and personal)

Describe your leadership style? Is your answer theoretical or drawn from practical experience of leading others?

_____

_____

Are you currently aiding in anyone's professional development? As a leader, what are you currently doing on a small scale that would be beneficial to your future vision or organization?

_____

_____

Have you begun sharing your dream and vision? Have others begun to express interest in being a part of such a work? Is there anything tangible keeping you from placing action behind the dream?

_____

_____

List each resource that you forecast you will need to ensure your success, i.e. finance, time, people, space, machinery, etc. Identify your gaps in resources and attach names or entities next to them. These names or entities should have the capacity to fill your gaps.

_____

_____

Reflections and Next Steps

(Keep it honest and personal)

As you delve into the process of reclaiming your POWER, it's normal that some aspects of the process resonate more than others. Likely, there were some that you thought, "that's exactly where I am!" and others that presented with greater challenge. All of that is very good. It's good to see yourself with increased clarity. It's good to take in confirmation of what you perceive to be your reality. And it's good to look squarely upon those aspects of your professional development that will require more work to overcome and/or embrace. Remember, you can't walk others through terrains that are unfamiliar, and you can't effectively lead others where you've never gone. So, as you pull together the five aspects of your POWER, resolve to boldly go *there* and grow.

Remember, "when we talk about POWERing up, we're talking about effectively pulling each of the five components together in a manner that positions you to excel, lead, and prosper." Are there any areas of your POWER that are weaker and need development? Those that you lead, are you prepared to aid them in their process of POWERing up to ensure that you have a succession plan for the work that you do?

Quote in Context~

"You do have a story inside you; it lies articulate and waiting to be written behind your silence and your suffering." -Ann Rice

Many companies, organizations, and movements are merely an extension or reflection of someone's story. I briefly touched upon how one's purpose may be closely related to traumatic and unpleasant experiences within life. In many cases, these are the experiences that give birth to purpose or provides preparation to walk in purpose. For many, the hidden story is waiting to be written and shared so that others may be impacted, and their lives changed. Someone once shared with me that "the power is in the secret." Once you expose the secret, the secret loses its power to manipulate your emotions, cause you to operate in fear, and slow your progress. There's a frustration that accompanies the suppression of those experiences that were intended to launch you into your individual greatness. This becomes one's silence and suffering.

CHAPTER SEVEN

emPOWERed

"One doesn't discover new lands without consenting to lose sight, for a very long time, of the shore." -Andre Gide

The most valuable aspect of this book is you and those like you who have handled its pages with an intent to make a difference in your life and world. The world not only needs dreamers, it needs visionaries who are able to see beyond themselves and fashion a means of leading others into something greater than who and what they presently are. A dream may exist without a plan of action. Therein lies its shortcoming. But when one is determined that today's dream is worthy of planning, development, and sharing then it comes alive and a vision is conceived.

The overarching purpose of this book is to issue a call to action to leaders to take their post firmly behind their vision for tomorrow, and further gather those who would be led so that a predestined greatness will be realized. Are you confident enough to declare yourself as a leader? And are you willing to step up and take the lead, for the sake of making a difference? Those two questions will thin the herd of readers, at least for a while. And here's a third question: are you determined to be a *good* leader?

It is a truth that there are many men and women who are in recognized, leadership roles, but they are not *good* leaders. My goal is that you will be equipped and prepared to accept authority and effectively possess and use your POWER to lead. It is not enough to have a title, because titles are a dime a dozen. The real value lies within those who do the work. So, I want you to be proficient in the practice of influencing those in your charge. Lastly, you need to be prepared to sustain the energy, commitment, and discipline required to see an initiative through to completion.

Taking back your POWER and reclaiming the best parts of who you are focuses on you. However, being truly emPOWERed requires that you turn your focus upon those that you lead. When one is confident in their purpose, is unique in their outlook, consistently exercising their wonder, is fully-charged with energy, and wisely tapping and committing their resources, he or she is effectively prepared to model servant leadership. So, let's take time out to explore next steps:

- Resolve to move your plans and initiatives forward;
- Press past the fear of risk and failure;
- Be a 21st Century leader; and
- Thrive in uncomfortable situations

It's Time to Move!

It's not wasted time; that time you spend working for or with someone else. Truth is, many people who start a business initiative do so while they are still employed. After all, it takes time to grow and develop a business and its customer base as well as gain followers. So, as many dreamers realize, maintaining employment becomes a necessity to maintain a livelihood, finance your initiative, and continue to build credibility and reputation. These moments are not a waste. However, they should not be confused with a false sense of security or a claim of comfort. Many will attest to a progressive impatience with what was the norm, a discomfort within the status quo, and an almost unexplainable agitation with the very things that used to inspire them. Guess what! It's time to move!

It was in the fall of 1999 that I decided that I would strike out on my own. In hindsight, I really wasn't prepared, but I was certainly ready to make a move. At the time, I was working at one of the country's leading wholesale liquidation companies within its accounting department. I'd been with the company for several years, but my employment experience had peaked roughly six months earlier and I was biding my time and paying my bills down to reduce my cost of living. I remember sharing my plans to resign my position with my mother, and she repeatedly encouraged me to hold on until I got another job. The problem that I had was that I didn't want another job. I wanted something more. I had a few clients, was being referred fairly regularly, and all signs seemed to point to that being my ideal time to depart and go another direction. That's exactly what I did, and I don't regret it.

It should be noted that there is a difference between being ready to move and being prepared to do so. Being ready is a mental and emotional resolve to discontinue one thing and pursue another. It's that part of you that can declare something as done even though you are legally tethered to it or committed in one respect or other. This is common in relationships or marriages, where one or both individuals have moved on mentally and emotionally long before the divorce is finalized. However, being prepared is when the groundwork has been laid for a complete transition from one state of being to the next. It's the execution of a plan to gather new and old resources and commit them to a new passion.

There's a trope that's parroted within Christian circles that "what God has for me is for me!" And there's *some* truth in that. There are times and events within life wherein there's a knowing that there is a specific path and course of action that is designed for one to travel. It's communicated by confirming voices that are outside of the individual's normal routine and establishes an assurance that there's a spiritual promise of something better or different that will manifest in the days ahead. "Days ahead" could be weeks, months, and even years into the future, as there is generally a period between the promise and the fulfillment. This period serves as time to prepare for a future opportunity.

What is unfortunate is when people who legitimately believe in their destiny fail to prepare for it. So, the door of opportunity opens in the fullness of time, but they are unable to walk through it, because they are ill-prepared to do so. What God has for them truly is for them, but because they were not prepared to walk through the open door, someone who was prepared for that level of opportunity walked through it instead, and walked away with life-changing benefits. Inaction is a coffin for dreams that have grown comfortable and sleep. Have you allowed your dreams to slumber?

Life seems to present windows of opportunity with inequity from one person to the next. Some people are fortunate to be presented with doors of opportunity repeatedly and with frequency, while others seem to be presented with doors only a few times throughout their lifetime. If one focuses on that reality, inaction and bitterness will likely be their story. One will be better served by asking two questions: Am I ready? And, am I prepared?

Are you simply biding your time, awaiting some sort of transition from where you are to where you envision you could be? If so, I want to share a secret with you. *The secret to getting ahead is getting started*. It's not an original thought. Mark Twain said it first. The words are no less true today than they were when his lips uttered them long ago.

You may have the greatest of dreams, the most beautiful vision, and the most detailed of plans, but it all comes to nothing if you never get started. Many will agree that the most difficult aspect of any new initiative is simply getting started; taking that first step outside of familiarity and into something unknown or unproven. Whether you succeed or fail, you will be neither the first nor the last to experience that reality. However, if you opt to settle for a personal status quo, your standard pat on the back for a job well done, and the artificial security of what's familiar, then you will fail those who would be followers of your vision; and the butterfly effect of your inaction upon the world will be immeasurable.

I want to challenge you to make daily progress toward building your dream and expressing your vision. Allow your actions to line up with your words, and further ensure that your words are expressions of your vision in one respect or other. Why? Because words have power, but you don't want to be all talk and no action; so, lead with action and people will hear you. Remember, you're emPOWERed, so you have everything that you need to be successful. You just need to move!

Take One Step, Then Two

Are you ready for a miracle? Seriously, are you ready? Are you *prepared* for one? I'll bet you're not asked that question often. I'm not talking about anything like the Red Sea parting or lepers being healed, but about something within your life that is no less miraculous. One definition of a miracle is "an amazing product or achievement, or an outstanding example of something.[4]" The problem with miracles is the perception of those who experience or witness them. There's the willingness to believe that miracles are most credible when they exist outside of oneself. Consider this thought. You experience a miracle each day. I'll give you an example.

Daily, people engage in an action that has been taken for granted as routine but is nothing short of a miracle—walking. Consider a baby as he takes his first steps. He's wobbly and unbalanced, arms outstretched, and knees lifting high. His goal is specific and seemingly every bit of his attention and energy is directed toward taking that next step toward something…anything. He's beginning a new chapter in his life; thousands of steps and dozens of falls. He's making progress, and once he clears this developmental hurdle, he'll never want to crawl again.

It is a truth that there are millions of men, women, boys, and girls who are unable to walk. In deference to them, I want to expand my example to assumptions that we make within our lives. It is because we assume things that we overlook the powerful and miraculous acts found within our daily routines. Consider this…each time that you take a step, you are literally throwing your body off-balance and catching yourself. The timing, collaboration of muscles and

---

[4] https://en.oxforddictionaries.com/definition/miracle

reflexes, and coordinated brain activity required to make this happen is nothing less than a miracle. As you repeatedly throw yourself off-balance and catch yourself, you enable your progression from point A to point B. Though you've done this thousands of times, you are not exempt from falling, as life reminds you that you aren't as far removed from that uncertain, wobbly baby with the determined eyes and outstretched hands.

The act of walking is no less an achievement today than it was when you were just a babe. Perhaps, there aren't any doting parents and grandparents clapping their hands and smiling exuberantly each time you do it, but that's only because it's an action that's taken for granted, until such an act becomes impossible.

The overarching truth is that you and I cannot progress from one place in life, business, relationships, education, etc. to another without being willing to throw ourselves off-balance to get there. If you want to transition from being an employee to being a business owner, you'll need to be willing to be off-balance from time to time. If you want to become a leader within your community, you'll need to be willing to be off-balance, even if just temporarily. Just as the repeated act of throwing yourself off-balance and catching yourself enables you to progress from one place to another, this mental resolve to take risks and chance failure is what enables you to progress from one level of professional development to another. Grow comfortable, and you're standing still. So, I want to a take few moments and coach that part of you that is risk-averse. Consider this:

1. ***Dreams aren't actualized in safe zones.*** There's a big world out there and, if you're risk-averse, it can become even bigger (and scarier) as you view it through the lens of fear. There are opportunities to be seized, but the bigger fish are in the deeper waters and the sweetest fruits hang from the highest limbs. If you want to explore your potential, you'll need to step outside of your personal and professional safe zones to begin the journey. When you're willing to chase your passions into unknown territories, you'll reap the greatest benefits.

2. ***Success is a pursuit, though not so trivial.*** Here is a reality to be mindful of: you don't know it all. Taking risks may place you in situations, circumstances, and opportunities that you didn't clearly foresee. Since you aren't an all-knowing individual, you will encounter situations wherein you don't know what to do or are uncertain of the next step. It's in those situations that you'll have to think, pray, and trust your way through it. If you're operating within your wheelhouse, you'll work it out. Expect to be successful but be open to becoming successful through means and avenues that lie outside of your plan.
3. ***Embracing risk-taking helps you overcome a fear of failure.*** For many, the fear of failure is a roadblock of their success. It's like a small voice in their head rehearsing all the worst outcomes and possible losses that may be realized by making the wrong decision. Each time you embrace risk-taking, you turn down the volume on that voice within your head and establish a practice of overcoming fear.
4. ***Risks are avenues of life lessons.*** Truly, this can be perceived in good and bad ways. So, let's reframe it to glean the value of this truth. New opportunities, lessons, and internal growth are the outcomes that are typically gained from being willing to take risks. There's no guarantee that there won't be painful experiences, but even they equip us with knowledge that we likely didn't have beforehand. In reality, risks are avenues of life lessons; so, avail yourself of this free education of sorts and learn.

I want to challenge you to press past those things that present themselves as barriers to your progress. Remember, being emPOWERed turns your focus upon those whom you serve—both customers and those you lead. With that in mind, you can't afford to lose time due to fear of the unknown, fear of failure, and hesitancy to move outside of comfort zones. Be willing to throw yourself off balance and catch yourself. Make it a practice and do it in a manner that others can see and study; one step, then two evidenced by progress and realized dreams.

The 21ˢᵗ Century Leader

There are countless books on many different aspects of leadership, including leadership styles, leadership theories, great leaders, leadership development, and the list goes on. If you choose to invest your time into really understanding not only the practice of leadership but the *culture* of leadership, then it won't take long for you to realize that there is no one-size fits all approach to leading people. You'll also notice that leadership and the practice of leading others has changed and continues to change.

I've invested time and energy within a few universities and training programs; so, I have a few diplomas hanging on a wall. My educational experiences have their value, but after achieving what I have, I've realized that my education didn't move the needle much one way or the other in my thinking concerning what is good management and those that I consider good leaders. More than my education, my approach to leading others has been shaped by mentors and former supervisors.

I've worked under a couple really good leaders in my career; leaders who modeled exemplary ideals, ethics, behaviors while pushing the merits and supporting the ideas of their subordinates. They were constantly developing their people into being prepared to take on leadership roles. We knew their vision and were committed to contributing toward its success. We weren't just titles or roles. We were people being led by a leader who understood the humanity of their team as well as the skill set. They captured my and my co-workers' respect, so we made the entirety of our talents available without mandate, but voluntarily and with excitement. I was a part of something bigger than myself and didn't feel exploited, taken for granted, or used. These were people demonstrated the difference between being a manager of others and being a leader.

In contrast to my experiences working with good leaders, I've also worked with others who were in leadership positions (by title), but simply supervised or managed their teams. These individuals were driven by the numbers and did whatever it took to meet performance measures; oftentimes done without regard for their team but rather at its expense. Managers use policies, regulations, rules, the voice of their superiors, and even their title to corral their team and drive performance, rather than legitimately gaining the respect of those who would do the work, and oftentimes fail to invest the time to mentor and develop others.

The good and bad leadership that I've worked under throughout my career has shaped both my thinking and leadership style. People, words, experiences, and the context of all of the above have a powerful influence upon how we develop as leaders, but it is our resolve to serve others through leadership that leaves us open to perpetually learning how to lead well. So, I challenge you to gather the tools that you need to consistently progress in your professional development. If you need a mentor, then get a mentor. If you need training, then seek and acquire training. If you need a degree, then enroll in school. You may not need any of these, or you may need them all. The question is, are you committed to putting in the work to acquire all that you need to be a *good* leader who leads well? People deserve leadership that encourages consistent growth and development. This is what lends toward an organization and its staff and leadership being prepared for the future and inevitable change.

Bill Gates once said, *"As we look ahead into the next century, leaders will be those who empower others."* There is a marked difference between power and authority. For example, authority is granted positionally. Because you are a Director over a division, you have the authority to hire new employees or terminate employment. Along with that authority, you possess the power to reassign workers, enforce policies, develop and implement initiatives, etc.

It is important to note that your power and authority should work in a complementary manner as you lead those under your charge. However, in many organizations, departments, and units, it does not happen in this way. Why? Because while authority is legally granted, power may be usurped by others, and even forfeited or given away to others. I've attended meetings where the manager of a unit was speaking and sharing information with staff, but there was an undercutting murmur in the back of the room that shared doubt, disbelief, and contrary directives. The person who initiated the sidebar commentary and even issued contrary directives was successful in doing so, because he or she possessed power within the unit.

Power within an organization, department, or unit is not legally granted as authority is. Power is granted over time by the person who should have it, i.e. the legal authority, or it is assumed by someone who can exert their influence over others. It is the person who is so respected and trusted that others feel that their credibility and ability to lead outweighs that of the person who actually holds the leadership position. So, staff hear the person in charge, but then they look to the person who really has the power to assess whether or not he or she is in agreement with what's been spoken before they move upon the directive. It may be the quietest voice in the room, but if that voice can influence others to move in concert with or contrary to the voice of the leader, then that quiet voice has taken possession of the leader's power.

This type of scenario is very common within large and small organizations, when the leadership has not been careful to take back and retain their POWER. A typical response by management is to uproot the contrary voice and those who would follow it. This type of organizational culling negatively impacts the relationship between leaders and followers and creates a "noise" within the organization that makes it difficult for even good leaders to be heard. The more effective response by leadership is to gain influence over the influencer; meaning, gain his or her respect and bring him or her in line with the vision. By doing so, the leader redirects the dissenting voice, so that it delivers the same message as what is communicated by leadership. Then that person becomes candidate number one for development into being a legitimate leader within the organization with legal authority to exercise their power.

Now, let's get back to Gates' future leader. He is careful to narrowly define the future leader. He doesn't bother with the concept of a *good* leader or *bad* leader, but simply suggests that those who empower others will be our leaders. This disregards those who hold leadership positions because of their title as well as those who pilfer power from those in leadership. Focusing on legitimate leaders, their qualifications are proven by their ability and willingness to empower those who choose to follow them. However idealistic, this definition of a leader is requiring for those who want to lead and places their followers exactly where they deserve to be—in a place to be served and developed by those who develop the vision.

So, you're emPOWERed. Congratulations! But there's a greater value to the reclamation of your best parts. You now have an opportunity (and responsibility) to emPOWER others. This act of paying it forward captures the heart of leadership while earning the respect of followers. You're the 21st century leader modeling leadership in a manner that is as unique as your personal brand—duplicable in practice and visible by design.

Seek Uncomfortable Situations

Years ago, I was going through interviews for a position at an accounting firm. Part of the firm's recruitment process was a series of screenings that included a credit check, background check, and a psychological profile. After the results of the screenings were received, one of the partners called me in to discuss items of interest to him. During our conversation, he disclosed two things. One was that, according to the results of the psychological profile, I am an individual who requires an organized work environment. I argued the validity of that conclusion, before we moved on to the second result. He then shared that the results of the profile noted that "this individual has an unusual ability to work within uncomfortable circumstances for an extended period of time." I didn't appreciate that truth until years later. In that vein of thought, let's discuss uncomfortable situations.

Contrary to popular belief, uncomfortable situations are not things to dread and avoid. In fact, they are circumstances that you should appreciate and seek. Why? Because it's life's uncomfortable situations that stretch us, cause us to call upon hidden resources, encourages us to think quickly, and teaches us the unexpected about ourselves and others. I'm not necessarily talking about embarrassing situations, although uncomfortable and embarrassing are oftentimes synonymous. I'm talking about situations that force us out of our comfort zones and challenges us to do something that we aren't prepared to do.

> *I like to play the grey areas in life - that's the most uncomfortable place to be. Nobody likes to be in that in-between state where they don't know what's going to happen. There's a lot of tension in that, and a lot of stuff to play with - where it's uncomfortable and awkward and sad and scary.* -Melanie Lynsky

See, we all have grey areas, but few actually like to play in their grey areas. Yours may not be mine and mine may not be yours, but we each have our own areas of discomfort that are likely areas of untapped potential, resources, and experiences. For a moment, think of one or two-word answers to the following question: What makes you uncomfortable?

Toss this question into a crowd of people and you'll get a seemingly unlimited list of words, that may include "change", "public speaking", "embarrassment", and "conflict" to name a few. Some of these same words may be what makes you uncomfortable, but you may have others that are all your own, based upon your personality, life experiences, etc. How about people groups and ethnicities? Might some of these make your list of one and two-word responses?

These words dwell and thrive outside of our mental and emotional safe zones in which we reside. Unfortunately, they rent real estate within the same neighborhoods as our opportunities. So, life offers us two choices:

1. Remain within the confines of our homes (safety zones); or
2. Venture outside into the neighborhood and chance encountering those things that make us uncomfortable.

I challenge you to seek uncomfortable situations and expose yourself to new opportunities and experiences that will increase your capacity. In time, you will note that none of these things—these aspects of life that make you bristle—have the power to confine you to your safety zones. It's the *fear* of these things that holds power over you, if you allow it. So, venture beyond your safe zone, be mindful of those things that make you uncomfortable when they present themselves and run full-speed to embrace each one. Fear will lose both its voice and its power, and you will gain increased comfort in expressing your emPOWERed, unique manner of leading, creating, and decision-making.

Your process has involved boldly reclaiming the best parts of who you are, but are you bold enough to seek out those things that would normally make you slow down, step back, or even retreat? If so, then list those things that make you uncomfortable. Remember, they are your opportunities' neighbors and they will likely introduce themselves as you venture into your professional and social neighborhood. So, venture beyond your safe zone, be mindful of those things that make you uncomfortable when they present themselves and run full-speed to embrace each one. Fear will lose both its voice and its power, and you will gain increased comfort in expressing your emPOWERed, unique manner of leading, creating, and decision-making. That's part of being emPOWERed, right? You can't be a trailblazer while fearing what's on the trail ahead. So, let's delve a little deeper and examine how you embody what being emPOWEREDed really means.

You are the leader, visionary, and dreamer that people not only need but want, and as such you are:

- **EmPOWERed to trust those who trust you to lead them.** You don't just want followers. You want those who follow you to grow and develop. Trust fertilizes the soil for their professional development. Trust that they have workable ideas and value their opinions. Trust that they will put forth their best efforts but give them room to fail and learn from their failures. If you're employing people, trust them to actually do their job. Don't micromanage. If they have the talent and skill set to obtain a position, then give them space and opportunity to do the work and freely express themselves through their performance. This will afford them freedom to grow and you will likely retain employees and followers.

- **EmPOWERed to show genuine respect for those you lead.** Respect goes a long way toward getting others to put forth their best efforts and work hard without micromanagement. Choose empathy over aggression. Recognize those who work hard and develop those who have potential but lag behind. Respect, liberally given, will create psychological safe zones and encourage workers, volunteers, and followers to take risks that will render immeasurable benefits to your team(s) and organization.

- **EmPOWERed to applaud the successes of those you lead.** Be the mentor and/or coach that your people need and rest in that role whenever required. Everyone appreciates acknowledgement for a job well done. With this in mind, when possible, address failures privately but acknowledge and celebrate successes publicly and often. This will foster a culture of positive reinforcement that employees will not only appreciate but replicate within their communications with one another.

- **EmPOWERed to be transparent and practice active listening.** You can roll a lot into this action. People appreciate honesty and transparency. Perfection isn't a requirement, but consistent authenticity will maintain the trust of those who follow you. Listening is a large part of communication, and active listening is a skill that must be honed and practiced. Foster confidence with each one of your followers that though they may be one voice among dozens, theirs is the only voice that's captured your full attention. More than anything, people want to be heard and coupled with that desire is their want to be understood. If you make a consistent effort to actively listen, the results will show in both individual and collective performance.

- **EmPOWERed to have and show genuine compassion for those you lead.** I touched on empathy earlier. Effective leaders have the ability to marry empathy with compassion in a manner that communicates a genuine concern for the person that extends well beyond their real or potential contribution to the vision. This is what fosters a family atmosphere within the workplace, as leaders express genuine compassion for those they lead, and their people in turn express genuine compassion for one another. Effectively and consistently done, a culture containing empathy and compassion allows for tough love to be readily accepted and hit its intended mark for needed correction.

As stated earlier, taking back your POWER and reclaiming the best parts of who you are focuses on you, but being emPOWERed turns the focus upon those whom you lead. Your desire to step outside of your personal and professional safe zones to start a business, an organization, a ministry, or a movement is great. But your resolve to place action behind that desire is worthy of applause. In a crowd of millions who would be satisfied with the way that their life and world are, you're one who is willing to take the lead and be the difference. So, pat yourself on the back. My only warning is that you not pat too long, because your resolve to be an emPOWERed leader is actually a declaration that it's not about you in both the short and long-run, and in big and small ways. It's all about serving others—clients, customers, communities, and those whom you lead.

Taking back your POWER is a process of self-assessment, adjustment, and preparation. The challenges within these chapters are placed before you to encourage you to take an honest and introspective look at the most important individual reading this book—you! Your dream lives and breathes with a deafening heartbeat that demands to be acknowledged, nurtured, and developed. Simply put, it's your time to begin a life-changing transition from being led to being the leader. This process acknowledges all that you bring to the fore and contribute to someone else's vision and work, because sometimes in the midst of working diligently you may overlook your own value, though someone else deems you to be invaluable to what they do.

Your understanding of your POWER and resolve to reclaim each component equips you to move independently within your vein of leadership. You are now emPOWERed, though not perfect. Perfection is an unrealistic expectation. You are qualified. Qualified for what? To be sure, you are qualified to lead through service that is self-sacrificing, exemplary, and models an invested greatness that is unique to who you are and benefits all who are served by it.

Reflections and Next Steps

(Keep it honest and personal)

How does service live within your personal and professional plan for your future? Who will you serve, and how will you serve them? Rather than thinking in terms of market share, how will you increase the number of people you and communities that you will serve?

_____

_____

_____

_____

List those things that make you uncomfortable? Identify those items that you are unable or unwilling to embrace. What's prohibiting you from addressing these items particularly?

_____

_____

_____

_____

Quote in Context~

"One doesn't discover new lands without consenting to lose sight, for a very long time, of the shore." -Andre Gide

It is arguable that nothing worth having comes easily. So, most who have an entrepreneurial charge, are driven by a call to leadership, or desires to model positive behaviors expect challenges and readily accept them as a part of the journey to their professional destination. The reality is amplified when one realizes that their dream or vision (their new lands) comes with required sacrifices to realize desired increases. The resolve to step outside of personal and professional safety zones (your shore) must be adopted not only willingly but whole-heartedly, as there is a passage of time between one's departure from one shore and arrival at another shore at the end of their journey.

In the context of taking on visible leadership, one must be willing to address and resolve personal doubts and uncertainties, maintain the clarity to make qualified, effective decisions, and avail themselves of opportunities to develop those who are willing to follow—many times, in a very private manner. Followers are oftentimes unaware that their leader has lost sight of the shore and has no idea when another shore (their destination) will be discovered. Yet, he or she leads through these periods of uncertainty with a visible confidence that instills respect, admiration, and loyalty by those who follow and put feet to the vision.

CONCLUSION

Martin Luther King, Jr. stated, *"If a man is called to be a street sweeper, he should sweep streets even as a Michelangelo painted, or Beethoven composed music or Shakespeare wrote poetry. He should sweep streets so well that all the hosts of heaven and earth will pause to say, 'Here lived a great street sweeper who did his job well.'"*

For many, that quote resonates within both their mind and spirit, because they feel that their work is a calling of sorts. It is their responsibility to fulfill what is set before them, to the best of their ability, and present it to another to continue after they've passed on. With such an approach to work and career, a great requirement accompanying the assigned task is that of preparation and being equipped.

As a consultant, I've had the opportunity to travel to Europe, Asia, Africa and to cities throughout the United States. I've been fortunate to meet and know many people with differing cultures and backgrounds. Among so many differences, there are striking similarities, one of which being a great desire had by talented people to develop personal endeavors, follow a calling, or pursue their destiny. With the passage of time, many have become fearful or discouraged. Thinking that their window of opportunity has long ago closed, they've remained tethered to people, businesses, ministries, and visions that are not their own. It is an artificial security that causes many to forsake the dream within, and this becomes a source of regret within time. It is my desire that you will allow my words to rain down hope upon your dying or withered dreams and that you will allow them to live again, just as you live, with every heartbeat growing stronger and your dissenting voices growing faint.

It is the role and responsibility of *good* leaders to recognize others with leadership potential and then further develop them to manage even greater works. Unfortunately, many have become pigeon-holed within roles that they've long outgrown, for the sake of retaining their value within their organization of employ. So, many who should be developing as new talent within a leadership capacity have been relegated to positions wherein their knowledge, gifts, talents, and skill sets are extracted, and another man's vision benefits. This brand of leadership is rendered by men and women who have not invested the time to become emPOWERed and lack the selfless nature that grows their organizations through service to those who serve others.

Perhaps, you are that talented individual who has been mishandled by leadership. My question to you concerns your resolve to identify next steps within your life—your decision specific to your circumstance. My call to action is not to those who are seeking recognition. It is to those who know within their knower that there is more for them—more to do, more to be, and more to achieve. This is your time.

So, I want to end this book with much the same message with which I began—you are POWERful. Makes no difference if you're six years old or 60; if you're college-educated or attended the school of hard knocks; if you're considered disabled or disadvantaged. There is still time for you to step out, fully-equipped, into your own work. There are still opportunities to make a difference in your life and within your world. You just need to take back your POWER!

I would like to place two more challenges before you; and that is for you to name the person, thing, or circumstance that serves as a barrier to you pursuing your destiny, call and purpose. Sometimes, the process of reclaiming the best parts of who you are requires that you first eliminate the worst parts—negative people and environments, complacency, and fears. You name it (literally) and begin to place action behind your deepest desires to be more and do more. Remember, all of the potential to be who you were created to be was already invested within you at your birth. Are you ready to stretch yourself and test those things that you believe about yourself deep down within? If so, then here is your second challenge:

Take a step. However small, take one step…then two.

SCRIPTURE REFERENCES

Chapter One
"And we know that all things work together for good to them that love God, to them who are the called according to *his* purpose" (Romans 8:28, KJV).

Chapter Three
"I will praise thee; for I am fearfully *and* wonderfully made: marvellous *are* thy works; and *that* my soul knoweth right well" (Psalm 139:14, KJV).

Chapter Four
"And the LORD answered me, and said, Write the vision, and make *it* plain upon tables, that he may run that readeth it" (Habakkuk 2:2, KJV).

Chapter Six
"A good name is more desirable than great riches; to be esteemed is better than silver or gold" (Proverbs 22:1, NIV).

"And the LORD answered me, and said, Write the vision, and make *it* plain upon tables, that he may run that readeth it" (Habakkuk 2:2, KJV).

GET TO KNOW M. STANLEY BUTLER

Dr. M. Stanley Butler is an author, teacher, and serial entrepreneur. With more than 25 years of experience as a financial and administrative leader within the private, public, and nonprofit sectors, he has effectively provided counsel and/or guidance to national and international organizations. Known as an "Infopreneur", Dr. Butler models servant leadership in a manner that builds, mentors, and prepares others to live with purpose and serve with excellence.

Dr. Butler is the founder of Striving Toward Excellence in Public Service (STEPS), Inc., a Maryland nonprofit providing developmental, financial and administrative services to nonprofits and small businesses. He is also the President of M. Stanley Enterprise & Ventures, LLC, through which he provides coaching and entrepreneurial training services to leaders and organizations throughout the United States.

Dr. Butler's publications are purposed to address personal and professional needs among people of faith. His books include "Take Back Your POWER! Boldly Reclaim the Best Parts of Who You Are", "Sometimes, Man's Rejection is God's Protection," "Between Pillars of Purpose", "Caleb's List: Funding Resource for Christian Nonprofits", and "Nonprofit Nuggets: Nonprofit Does Not Mean Nonprofitable". He is an active blogger, a contributing writer for numerous Christian magazines, and facilitates a Leadership Excellence series of courses through his nonprofit organization at **www.stepsofleadership.org** and **www.stepsinstituteonline.org**.

M. Stanley Butler is available for conferences, workshops, and entrepreneurial coaching.

Contact him at:
M. Stanley Enterprise & Ventures, LLC
100 Centennial Avenue #73, La Plata, MD 20646
Phone: (877) 447-0900 Email: drbutler@mstanleybutler.com

Join Dr. Butler's mailing list at www.mstanleybutler.com or you may connect with him on
social media at:

Facebook | https://www.facebook.com/drmstanleybutler
POWER Up! Group | https://www.facebook.com/groups/POWERup2019/
Twitter | https://twitter.com/mstanleybutler
Instagram | mstanleybutler

LEADING THROUGH SERVICE

DON'T MISS THESE TITLES BY M. STANLEY BUTLER

Sometimes, Man's Rejection is God's Protection

Dr. M. Stanley Butler tackles difficult aspects of rejection, common to many of us—perhaps, common to you—and reveals that even these things are a small part of a greater purpose and design. With an application of spiritual truths, he empowers you to excel and overcome in spite of those who have failed to realize your true value and potential. Your enemy desires that you would be rejected and embittered, but even these things cannot derail your purpose or your destiny, because none of it occurs to God. He watches over a plan whose end was declared from the beginning and ensures that every failed relationship, act of abuse, and unfulfilled promise works for your good. There are victories you have yet to realize, and God is waiting to reveal this truth…Sometimes, Man's Rejection Is God's Protection!

www.ingramcontent.com/pod-product-compliance
Lightning Source LLC
Chambersburg PA
CBHW071004080526
44587CB00015B/2334